"Ours is a faith that is not merely intellectual. It is meant to be lived out in the sometimes beautiful, sometimes terrible physical world we inhabit. Our hope is that Discipler helps you build the spiritual muscles that lead to a healthier life in Christ, and that, thus empowered, you are ready and eager for the good work of changing your local churches, and thereby changing your communities and changing the world."

DISCIPLER

An Interactive Guide to
Intentional, Relational, Accountable Discipleship

PHIL MAYNARD
AND EDDIE PIPKIN

Market
Square
BOOKS

Discipler

An Interactive Guide to
Intentional, Relational, Accountable Discipleship

©2017 Phil Maynard
books@marketsquarebooks.com
P.O. Box 23664   Knoxville, Tennessee 37933

ISBN10: 0-9987546-3-3
ISBN13: 978-0-9987546-3-5
Library of Congress: 2017951765

Printed and Bound in the United States of America

Cover Design ©2017 Market Square Publishing, LLC

DISCIPLER INTRODUCTION

As we began our work at Excellence in Ministry Coaching (EMC3), our goal was to use our decades of ministry experience to produce practical discipleship tools. When we visited congregational leaders around the country, we found passionate, motivated followers of Christ. They had faithfully attended Bible Studies, small groups, and countless committee meetings. They had read books, watched videos, and attended scores of training sessions. They had embraced the concepts of growth-focused congregational leadership: the call to discipleship; the call to connect meaningfully with their own communities; the call to build relationships that transform the world.

At workshops in which we reinforced the theological framework for these callings, we would inevitably see heads nodding in agreement. Local churches were hungry for this kind of challenge. Again and again, however, we heard the same question: *How?*

"We understand what Jesus is calling us to," these leaders were saying. "We understand the value of starting in our own backyard as we answer that call. We understand the destination. What we don't understand is how to get there."

It's like unpacking the box for a new bicycle on Christmas morning. They get the concept (two-wheeled, human-powered conveyance). They embrace the reason for its existence (cheap, fun transport). They understand the basic physics underlying the way the parts are connected (chains turn sprockets that turn wheels that pass over the ground on inflated tubes). But they sit there all morning, wistfully looking over the unassembled pieces because they don't have the proper tools for putting the thing together.

Well, here's your toolkit.

At EMC3, we first wrote a book (and accompanying workshop) called *Shift*, that shared the attitudes and approaches being embraced by growing and vibrant congregations, even in the face of a historic cultural pivot away from traditional church attendance. One such necessary shift is the movement from membership to discipleship. "Great," our workshop attendees said. "How do we do that?" So, we wrote a book (and accompanying workshop) called *Membership to Discipleship*, and we gave them tools for helping people navigate this process. One essential element of that process was helping people understand our call as Christ followers to make connections with friends and neighbors in order to share God's grace with them in life-changing ways. "Great," our workshop attendees said. "We agree! So, how do we do that?" And in response we wrote our *Connect!* materials (and accompanying workshop).

You get the idea. It's been a wonderful mind-and-heart-expanding process. And it's why we've written *Discipler*. This new book offers a very specific toolkit to help those who wish to follow Christ. In our previous materials we have shared the six ways in which our lives develop more fully as we know Christ more deeply (worship, hospitality, openness, obedience, service, and generosity). This book offers daily interactive exercises which explore these six areas for growth. They are sometimes reflective, sometimes hands-on experiences, sometimes provocative, sometimes comforting reassurances as to our true identity as children of God. At all times they are moving us toward the goal of a deeper relationship with our Lord and Savior.

Ours is a faith that is not merely intellectual. It is meant to be lived out in the sometimes beautiful, sometimes terrible physical world we inhabit. A strong faith is a robust faith, lived with joy but ready for the reality of challenges and troubles. Our hope is that *Discipler* helps you build the spiritual muscles that lead to a healthier life in Christ, and that, thus empowered, you are ready and eager for the good work of changing your local churches, and thereby changing your communities and changing the world.

Godspeed,

Phil Maynard and Eddie Pipkin,
EMC3 (Excellence in Ministry Coaching)

August 2017

WHAT IS DISCIPLESHIP?

Discipler is designed to provide a daily practical guide with Scripture-based reflections and exercises that will help you grow towards maturity as a disciple of Jesus Christ. We begin with these fundamental questions:

- What is a disciple?
- What does a disciple of Jesus Christ do?

It is helpful to answer these essential questions by returning to the words of Jesus, himself, as recorded in Matthew 4:19...

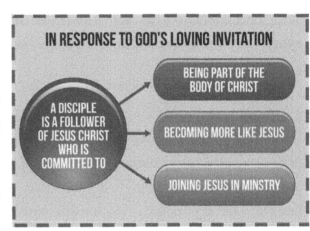

<u>Follow me</u> (making a choice to be part of the body of Christ)
<u>And I will make you</u> (becoming more like Jesus)
<u>Fishers of men</u> (joining Jesus and his followers in ministry).

There are many different kinds of disciples at work in the world, but the discipleship characterized as following Jesus is unique. One may be a dedicated admirer of the ideas of a very learned person, or one may be passionate about a particular strand of philosophy. This means adhering to a set of ideas or ideals, but what we're talking about in the case of following Jesus is adopting a lifestyle—a way of living—that emulates Jesus in each moment, in every decision as to how we speak and act.

Discipleship is a continuing journey into the abundant life for which we were created. It is a process of continual development through which we grow in maturity (becoming more Christ-centered and fully surrendered). In a culture obsessed with end results and perfection, it's crucial to remember that, for a disciple, it's the journey itself that is most important. Disciples are often described as 'learners', but this is only one, potentially limited, understanding of discipleship. Discipleship in the biblical tradition is not just learning <u>about</u> Jesus; it means becoming more <u>like</u> Jesus—doing life the way Jesus did life.

There is no one-size-fits-all for this journey of discipleship. Each of us is uniquely wired to serve our purpose, and part of the journey is figuring out our strengths and weaknesses and exactly where we fit in. Choosing to be part of the body of Christ, working to become more like Jesus, and joining fellow Christ-followers in ministry are all broad strokes. They allow for unlimited possibilities for how your particular life of discipleship flourishes.

In order to understand how this process plays out, we look closely at the Gospel accounts of the life of Jesus and those who would follow him, and we can clearly identify six dimensions for discipleship (it is in the details within each of these dimensions that our own individual story comes to life):

A Life of Worship – A Life of Worship means participation in corporate worship, but it also includes personal worship (e.g. daily devotional time) and eventually an entire lifestyle of worship in which every action and circumstance becomes an opportunity to give glory to God.

A Life of Hospitality – A Life of Hospitality includes the traditional roles of being part of the church community and welcoming new people to worship, but it also includes our personal relationships with (and our acceptance of) people who are outside the church and potentially quite unlike us, even to the point of intentionally building relationships with people beyond the church in order to embody Christ's love for them.

A Life of Opening to Jesus – A Life Opening to Jesus points us in the direction of spiritual practices, such as Scriptural engagement and prayer, which help us to develop an awareness of the presence of Christ. This dimension of discipleship is focused on helping us develop an awareness of God's grace at work in our world and to place us in a position to receive and respond to that grace, that working of the Spirit.

A Life of Obeying Jesus – A Life of Obeying Jesus begins with our acceptance of a relationship with Jesus and our commitment to becoming like Jesus. As we move toward maturity, we begin to apply the teachings of Scripture to our own lives, and we develop partnerships with others to help them grow as disciples.

A Life of Service – A Life of Service includes supporting the ministry of the local church with our time and energy, as well as participating in service projects sponsored by the church, but it also includes a lifestyle of investing the best of who we are in service to others.

A Life of Generosity – A Life of Generosity includes presenting our tithes and offerings as an act of worship, but it also includes creating a lifestyle with margin that allows us to respond to the needs of others God puts in our path on a daily basis. It helps us think differently about the resources with which we have been entrusted.

Within each category of these dimensions of discipleship, we hopefully grow. If we are diligent, focused, and maintain healthy habits, we experience a progression of growth that can be described in stages which parallel the physical and intellectual growth of human beings as they move from infancy through childhood and adolescence to maturity.

Here are the five stages of spiritual development:

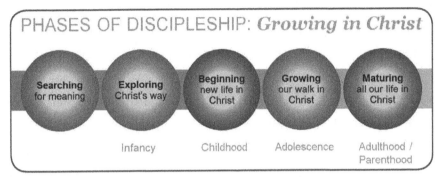

Searching – We all seek to make sense of our lives, asking questions like "What gives my life purpose, joy, and fulfillment?" We may seek to fill this fundamental longing in many different ways. [Note that for the purposes of Discipler, we don't deal with the 'searching' phase, because we assume that you must be at least at the 'exploring' phase if you are actively engaging the book's exercises.]

Exploring – We may attend church and want to belong, but we might not yet have committed to following Jesus. We may wrestle intellectually with God's presence in our lives, often with more caution that curiosity.

Beginning – We are beginning to understand and put into practice our newfound faith. Growth can be awkward. We are often vulnerable to insecurity and doubt. We can also be the most excited about faith at this stage. This is the largest and most active segment of congregants involved in church activities.

Growing – We are eager to be identified as Christians and going public with our faith. We are increasingly willing to take personal responsibility for our growing relationship with Jesus. We seek to integrate our faith into life in a holistic way, and we look to Jesus to help us live our day-to-day lives.

Maturing – We are moving toward complete surrender of our lives to Jesus. We exist to *know*, *love*, *obey*, *serve*, and *be with* Jesus. We also realize that the role of a disciple is to help make other disciples, and we live towards that goal.

It is important to note that, not only does progress happen in phases, and that different people will find themselves at different points along the path towards maturity, but also that different disciples will find themselves at different stages within the individual dimensions of discipleship (worship, hospitality, obedience, etc.). For example, a person may have a great passion for serving others (a characteristic associated with the 'growing' phase of the 'service' dimension), but they may simultaneously be only in the 'beginning' phase of 'opening to Jesus'. They may have expressed their intention to develop the spiritual disciplines which will deepen their connection to Jesus, but they may not yet have taken on the actual habits and attitudes that accurately describe a person in the 'growing' phase of that dimension of discipleship.

People will grow at different rates within the different dimensions of discipleship. This is dependent on the spiritual gifts with which God has uniquely endowed us, as well as our natural personality traits and interests. If you're a people person, you might naturally live out hospitality, even as you're struggling with generosity. If you're a natural introvert, you might have a good fit with worship, obedience, or even generosity, but struggle with service. That's okay, and it's normal. And, frankly, to some degree these imbalances in growth are the result of poor structures within our churches—we can have a lot of organized opportunities to serve, but fall short in creating engaging opportunities to study or pray. If we are to fully mature as disciples, however, we must strive to grow in each of these areas.

In order to have an honest view of that growth, it is important to move beyond generic descriptions of what that growth looks like, and instead understand the specific attitudes and actions which characterize each phase of development within each dimension of discipleship. That is what the *Discipler* material uniquely provides: exercises that explore each of these phases within each dimension. Having thoughtfully completed all exercises for each section, we grow a little deeper in the life to which Christ has called us.

Not a Solo Effort

The exercises in *Discipler* are designed to be experienced under the guidance of a mentor or spiritual director. This is a person who is mature in their discipleship and can, by virtue of their accrued wisdom and experience, help you process the daily exercises. This partner on your journey of spiritual growth will hold you accountable, challenge you when you need it, help you clarify your feelings, and celebrate your progress. This person should be carefully selected: someone with whom you share natural affinities, but not just a 'buddy'—they should be someone whom you admire as an inspiration in living out the life of faith. They should be someone who is willing and able to commit to this process, who will take it seriously and invest themselves in you. If you need help identifying such a person, your pastor or congregational spiritual growth leaders can help.

It is also possible to use the *Discipler* material as part of a small group process, with like-minded people interested in spiritual growth, under the leadership of a spiritual director or mentor. Using this approach, your group would meet regularly, sharing your experiences, insights, and questions.

Flexibility Is Important

The *Discipler* exercises are meant to be uniquely flexible. You will see that they are arranged in such a way as to give you six weeks' worth of exercises for each of the growth phases (exploring, beginning, growing, and maturing, if you were able to do one activity per day). Within each section there are six activities, one for each dimension of discipleship (worship, hospitality, openness to Jesus, obedience, service, and generosity). That leaves you a day for Sabbath in each week.

This format is a template to keep you focused and moving forward. It's not supposed to be a straightjacket to make you feel intimidated. It's a tool for your encouragement, so feel empowered to modify it in whatever manner works best for you (in consultation with your accountability partner or small group). But if your schedule means you need to take more time to complete a section, you might decide to give yourself two weeks to complete that section, etc.

For maximum potential progress, however, keep these suggestions in mind:

- It is okay to scan ahead and preview upcoming activities. In fact, it will likely be helpful, because some activities require more complex planning and scheduling.

- Treat each section's exercises as a unit, and complete that section before moving to the next unit. It's not necessary to stay on a strict daily schedule if that doesn't work for you. It is also not necessary to do the activities in order during a given section. Move them around as needed (some require a field trip or getting together with another person). BUT it is important to do all of the activities for that section before moving on to the next. Some of the activities are much more involved than others. If you can't complete an activity with the time constraints of a given section, brainstorm a plan for when and how you will accomplish it and talk those plans over with your mentor or group. Come back to those experiences at a later date if you need to.

- Try to meet with your mentor/spiritual director or *Discipler* small group once a week, or at a minimum once every two weeks. This is a critical part of your progress, and you should do everything that you can to make sure that these sessions happen. You and your mentor / spiritual director / small group can not only can not only talk about individual activities and your responses, but also develop an agreed upon plan for your completion schedule and any additional ideas you might want to try.

- If followed strictly, it will take six months to complete the *Discipler* activities, but you may stretch this out to a schedule that works for you and your spiritual partner or small group. It short-circuits the process to try to condense it into a shorter timeframe, however.

Keys for Success

Remember, this is a flexible, Scripture-based approach that is designed to guide you on a personalized journey. Our experience is that you will enjoy the greatest progress if you remember these guidelines:

- <u>Work with a guide</u>: You are far more likely to hold yourself accountable to the process and to gain greater wisdom and insight if you have a partner or partners for this journey who have already travelled this path. You can process the *Discipler* material one-to-one with a mentor or you can process it as part of small group with a leader who functions as group mentor.

- <u>Do things in order</u>: We have ordered the sections and activities so that they build upon a foundation of specific skills and insights. It will be tempting to skip over things that are difficult for you or unappealing, but to do so will deprive you of deeper spiritual truths.

- <u>Be flexible but diligent</u>: Don't be afraid to mix things up as needed to work with your unique life situation and the opportunities provided by your local congregation and the experiences of your spiritual mentor, but don't be willy-nilly in your approach. Have an agreed upon plan and be faithful to it.

- <u>Write down your reflections</u>: Writing down your observations, insights, and questions will be a crucial part of the process. It requires you to be more thoughtful, and it provides a written record of your progress that will be invaluable as you reflect back on your journey. In your reflections, don't be limited by the provided blank lines on the page for each exercise. That space is limited by publishing constraints. It's a great idea to have a second journal with blank pages to expand on your thoughts and ideas as you go.

- <u>Don't skimp, scrimp, or skulk</u>: Don't shortchange yourself by taking shortcuts, checking items off without fully engaging the activity, or being less than truthful with your spiritual mentor or small group partners. You will get out of this process whatever you put into it.

- <u>Don't be afraid to wander where the Spirit leads</u>: A particular activity may lead you to a deeper exploration of a passage of Scripture, a personal revelation you need to explore, or a desire to serve in a way you haven't before. Go for it! Modify and add to activities—create your own pages, your own chapters in your personal journey of discipleship discovery.

How to Use This Material in a One-to-one Conversation

Suggested time frame: 30 - 60 minutes
Location: Keep it casual, like at a café, coffee shop, park or back porch.

Connect Time

This is a time devoted to 'catching up' on life, following up on commitments made in previous sessions, and building the relationship.

Reflection and Accountability:

The majority of this time will be centered around the *Discipler* materials.

- As the conversation begins, ask, "As you interacted with the materials from the last section, where did you encounter a new idea or an activity that invited you to think about that dimension of discipleship in a new way?"

- Follow this opening conversation with the opportunity to share responses to each of the dimensions of discipleship growth, one at a time (worship, hospitality, opening to Jesus, obeying Jesus, service, and generosity). Share the goal for growth within each dimension's activity and the Scripture used for each reflection.

- Often, the conversation around responses will create an even deeper level of exploration around a particular theme. For example, a conversation around how the offering is introduced in worship might spark a deeper conversation about tithing and why we give in the first place. These deeper explorations are encouraged (even though they might preview down-the-road activities). Just remember to leave time for all the dimensions of growth to be covered.

Next Steps

As the meeting time concludes, invite your partner to consider what they are going to do with what they are discovering about growing as a disciple of Jesus this next week. You might frame the invitation like this: "As you consider the reflections on discipleship for this week, what next step is God inviting you to take in your journey toward maturity?"

Preview the next section, talking about any adjustments you need to make to timing or activities, and settling on a schedule for your next session.

Prayer Requests

Close the meeting time with an opportunity for partners to share prayer requests. Close with a time of prayer, giving attention to those shared requests.

How to Use This Material in a Small Group Setting

Suggested time frame: 60 - 90 minutes
Location: If possible, a casual and comfortable setting (as opposed to a sterile Sunday School room context). Someone's home or a private room at a local diner, etc.

Fellowship Time

As the group gathers, include a time for relationship building with the opportunity to share about what's going on in life (other than the coursework). It is helpful to have some light refreshments for people to enjoy as they reconnect with each other.

Worship Time

Groups are encouraged to have a brief time of worship as they reconnect with God. This might include:

- Song of Praise
- Brief devotional built on one of the dimensions of discipleship
- Opening prayer

Reflection and Accountability

The majority of the group meeting time will be centered around the *Discipler* materials.

- As the conversation begins, ask, "As you interacted with the activities from the last section, where did you encounter a new idea or an action that invited you to think about that a dimension of discipleship in a new way?"

- Follow this opening exchange with the opportunity to explore each individual dimension of growth, prompting each participant to share their own responses to each of the dimensions (worship, hospitality, being open to Jesus, being obedient to Jesus, service, and generosity). Get started by reviewing the goal for each dimension's activity and the Scripture used for reflection. For example: "Let's hear from each other how we responded to the activity focused on worship this week." Give all members of the group an opportunity to respond. Then move on to the next dimension.

- Often, the responses will create an even deeper exploration of a particular theme. For example, a group exchange around how the offering was introduced during a worship service might spark a deeper conversation about tithing and why we give in the first place. These conversations are encouraged (even though they may preview activities from later sections). Just remember to leave adequate time to cover all the dimensions of growth.

Next Steps

As the meeting time concludes, invite participants to consider what they are going to do with what they are discovering about growing as a disciple of Jesus this next week. You might frame the invitation like this: "As you consider the reflections on discipleship for the activities we just completed, what next step is God inviting you to take in your journey toward maturity?" Not all people will be comfortable responding to this question openly with the group, but you can encourage them to respond by saying, "Is there anyone who would like to share with us that next step?"

Also, preview the activities of the next section in the book, making any required adjustments to activities or schedule and clarifying your next meeting time and location.

Prayers for the Group

Close the meeting time with an opportunity for participants to share prayer requests. Note these requests and close with a time of prayer.

Enhancing the Group Experience: Communication

You will find it helpful to do an email reminder about the group meeting time, focus of that particular meeting, and prayer requests that were shared.

Enhancing the Group Experience: Sharing Meals Together

Groups often find that sharing a meal together (regularly or periodically) is a great way to build relationships and trust within the group. These, of course, are the foundational elements to creating space for deep, transparent, and vulnerable conversations that transform lives.

Enhancing the Group Experience: Serving Together

Each group is encouraged to find a way to serve together each month. Your church can probably provide you with a variety of opportunities to engage in ministry together out in the community. This provides a safe place for participants to explore how they are gifted to serve, as well as providing another great opportunity to build relationships within the group.

Facilitator Note: It is recommended that you scan ahead several weeks looking through the materials. There are occasions where some advance planning would be helpful as disciples are encouraged to serve both inside and outside of the church. You might assist in making these arrangements.

EXPLORING

∿ ∿ ∿ ∿ ∿

Part 1

Activity 1:
Exploring Worship

 **WORSHIP**

 GOAL: Consider the act of praise.

> *Let us not give up meeting together, as some are in the habit of doing, but encourage one another—and all the more as you see the Day approaching. —Hebrews 10:25 (NIV)*

 ACTION: Corporate Worship is a time when the community of faith gathers to celebrate how God has been at work in their midst; to praise God for the blessings received; to learn how to live as the people of God; and to offer themselves to the work God has called them to do. This week, experience a worship service and pay particular attention to the ways in which the community of faith offers praise to God. Such praise might be expressed in the words spoken, the songs sung, the body postures, the resources shared, and commitments made. Make notes of your observations during or immediately after the service. With what did you connect deeply?

_____

_____

_____

_____

 JOURNAL REFLECTION: Record your observations and reflections. Note specific ways in which you saw people expressing praise. In what ways did you feel you were sharing praise (internally and externally)?

_____

_____

_____

_____

_____

Activity 2: Exploring Hospitality

 HOSPITALITY

 GOAL: Observe hospitality to you (and others) in a worship setting.

> *This is how love is made complete among us so that we will have confidence on the day of judgment: In this world we are like Jesus... And he has given us this command: Anyone who loves God must also love their brother and sister.* —1 John 4:17-21 (NIV)

 ACTION: Following your participation in corporate worship from Activity 1, reflect on your experience of being welcomed. For example: Did someone have an actual conversation with you? Were you invited to share in refreshments or to join someone for lunch? Did you get introduced to the pastor or a staff member? Were you provided with additional resources and a clear path for obtaining more information and connecting to ministry?

_____

_____

_____

_____

 JOURNAL REFLECTION: As you think about your experience consider the question: Did I feel accepted and like I could belong to this community? How did you experience the love of God through the people in this community of faith? Write down your reflections. Make a list of the ways you felt welcomed, and a corresponding list of any ways you felt uncomfortable.

_____

_____

_____

_____

_____

_____

_____

Activity 3: Exploring Being Open to Jesus

OPENING TO JESUS

GOAL: Sense God's presence in the natural world.

> *O Lord, our Lord*
> *How majestic is your name in all the earth!*
> *You have set your glory above the heavens.* —Psalm 8:1 (NIV)

ACTION: Take a few minutes to enjoy a sunrise (or a sunset if you are not a morning person). Bask in the beauty of the moment. Enjoy the spectrum of colors provided. Notice the clouds moving slowly as the wind pushes them along.

JOURNAL REFLECTION: What feelings washed over you as you experienced the sunrise or sunset? Pleasure, thankfulness, joy? The Bible's authors record numerous reflections on God's majesty and creative care in the Scriptures (such as the Psalm quoted above.) Consider the God who brought such gifts into being. What specific things does this tell you about who God is?

_____

_____

_____

_____

_____

_____

_____

_____

_____

_____

Activity 4:
Exploring Obedience

 | OBEDIENCE

GOAL: Personalize the Good News.

> *For God so loved the world that he gave his one and only Son, that whoever believes in him shall not perish but have eternal life. —John 3:16 (NIV)*

ACTION: This verse from the Gospel of John is one of the most famous passages in the Bible. The word gospel means "good news." This particular verse is certainly good news for everyone, everywhere!

Read the verse through again a couple of times, slowly and thoughtfully. . . .

Now read it again, putting your name in place of the word "world":

This is how much God loved _____: He gave his Son, his one and only Son. And this is why: so that _____ need not be destroyed; by believing in him, _____ can have a whole and lasting life.

JOURNAL REFLECTION: Above all else, God, the creator of the universe, has chosen to love you and offers you a whole and lasting life. Consider the magnitude of that statement. How does this make you feel? Record your reflections.

_____

_____

_____

_____

_____

_____

_____

Activity 5: Exploring Service

SERVICE

GOAL: Discover real world examples of service.

Let no one seek his own good, but that of his neighbor. —1 Corinthians 10:24 (NIV)

ACTION: Oftentimes it feels like the world is filled with bad news. And yet there always seem to be examples of people making a positive difference (helping others, taking care of the world, seeking justice) if we take the time to look for them. Go to an online news compilation site such as Google News or Yahoo News and type in a search term like "serving others" or "good deed" and see if you can find an example of someone or some group making a difference in people's lives or in the community.

JOURNAL REFLECTION: What did the person or group do? What are they hoping to accomplish? What was your response when you read about this? How is the news article a witness of seeking good for a "neighbor"? How do the choices made by the people in this article reflect the Apostle Paul's guidance from the 1 Corinthians Scripture above?

_____

_____

_____

_____

_____

_____

_____

_____

_____

_____

Activity 6: Exploring Generosity

 | GENEROSITY

GOAL: Reflect on generosity in emergencies.

> *One person gives freely, yet gains even more; another withholds unduly, but comes to poverty. —Proverbs 11:24 (NIV)*

ACTION: Phil was getting ready to lead a workshop for a group of churches in Eastland, Texas when word was received that a family in the community had just lost everything due to a fire in their home. He says, "Our immediate response was an outpouring of care and concern for this family that none of us even knew. We took up a financial collection and raised several hundred dollars. The church family helped arrange temporary housing and food. The pastor went to meet with the family to determine how else the church could help in this time of need."

JOURNAL REFLECTION: Most of us have had the experience of reaching out to someone in need and sharing our time and resources. Write down an example of this from your own life. How did it make you feel to be in a position to help someone?

_____

_____

_____

_____

_____

_____

_____

_____

_____

_____

EXPLORING

Part 2

Activity 1:
Exploring Worship

WORSHIP

GOAL: Consider the impact of the pastoral message.

> *I became a servant of this gospel by the gift of God's grace given me through the working of his power. Although I am less than the least of all the Lord's people, this grace was given me: to preach to the Gentiles the boundless riches of Christ, and to make plain to everyone the administration of this mystery, which for ages past was kept hidden in God, who created all things. —Ephesians 3:7-9 (NIV)*

ACTION: As you attend corporate worship this week (that's worship with other people), we invite you to notice that there are a couple of distinct focus areas. First, as you discovered in Part 1, there is a focus on offering our praise to God. This, of course, takes many forms. Second, there is a focus on helping us learn how to take our next steps toward maturity as disciples (the message or sermon offered by the pastor) and opportunities that are provided to respond to the invitation to move forward (challenges for how we will offer our time, talents and resources, as well as opportunities for prayer, communion, etc.).

This week you are encouraged to pay particular attention to the message (sermon) presented during worship.

JOURNAL REFLECTION: How were you encouraged to honor God by the way you live? What, specifically, is the next step you were being asked to consider? What made the sermon effective in thinking about these questions? What, if anything, made you uncomfortable?

_____

_____

_____

_____

_____

Activity 2:
Exploring Hospitality

 HOSPITALITY

 GOAL: Remember your own story, how you were introduced to Jesus.

> *The next day Jesus decided to leave for Galilee. Finding Philip, he said to him, "Follow me." Philip, like Andrew and Peter, was from the town of Bethsaida. Philip found Nathanael and told him, "We have found the one Moses wrote about in the Law, and about whom the prophets also wrote—Jesus of Nazareth, the son of Joseph." "Nazareth! Can anything good come from there?" Nathanael asked. "Come and see," said Philip. When Jesus saw Nathanael approaching, he said of him, "Here truly is an Israelite in whom there is no deceit." "How do you know me?" Nathanael asked. Jesus answered, "I saw you while you were still under the fig tree before Philip called you." Then Nathanael declared, "Rabbi, you are the Son of God; you are the king of Israel." Jesus said, "You believe because I told you I saw you under the fig tree. You will see greater things than that." —John 1:43-50 (NIV)*

 ACTION: In the Gospel of John, chapter 1, we read the account of Philip inviting Nathanael to come and meet Jesus. Nathanael was a little reluctant to meet Jesus, but in doing so he discovered the purpose he had been looking for all his life.

 JOURNAL REFLECTION: Who introduced you to Jesus? Who invited you to church? What is the story of how you found your way to Christ and the people who were part of that process?

_____

_____

_____

_____

_____

_____

_____

Activity 3: Exploring Being Open to Jesus

OPENING TO JESUS

GOAL: Learn from someone else's story.

Listen to advice and accept discipline, and at the end you will be counted among the wise. —Proverbs 19:20 (NIV)

ACTION: There are lots of ways one can discover the difference that a relationship with God through Jesus makes. There are scores of books available. Lots of blogs are out there to read. Conferences are held all around the country helping people discover the power of this relationship. Perhaps the easiest and most natural is to ask a disciple you know and respect or someone you just met whose passion for Jesus impressed you. You are encouraged to take a disciple to lunch, coffee, or ice cream and ask them about their story.

- How did they meet Jesus?
- What difference is Jesus making in their life?
- How do they experience the presence of God?
- What are they doing to keep growing in that relationship?

JOURNAL REFLECTION: Record what you are learning and what questions are coming to mind as you reflect on this person's responses.

_____

_____

_____

_____

_____

_____

_____

_____

Activity 4:
Exploring Obedience

OBEDIENCE

GOAL: Perform a Random Act of Kindness.

> *Therefore, I urge you, brothers and sisters, in view of God's mercy, to offer your bodies as a living sacrifice, holy and pleasing to God — this is your true and proper worship.*
> *—Romans 12:1 (NIV)*

ACTION: Recently Phil was driving to an event in New Hampshire and came to a toll booth on the interstate. As he moved his car up to pay the toll, the toll booth operator informed him that the lady in the car ahead of him had paid his toll. To say the least, he was surprised and feeling "warm fuzzies" at the kindness that had been displayed.

Our culture calls actions like this "Random Acts of Kindness." The Scriptures call them service and generosity and even worship (refer back to Paul's words in his letter to the Romans). Perform an act of kindness (service, generosity, worship) this week in such a way that it is truly anonymous.

JOURNAL REFLECTION: What did you do? How did it make you feel? What surprised you the most about this experience?

_____

_____

_____

_____

_____

_____

_____

_____

Activity 5:
Exploring Service

SERVICE

GOAL: Consider ways you can serve in the context of your home faith community.

> *But be sure to fear the LORD and serve him faithfully with all your heart; consider what great things he has done for you.* — 1 Samuel 12:24 (NIV)

ACTION: Take a copy of the church bulletin and newsletter (or review the church website). How is this congregation involved in serving others? Look for ways that needs are met and, in particular, ways that the congregational participants are involved directly in serving.

JOURNAL REFLECTION: What did you discover? List ways that this congregation serves. What does this tell you about the heart of this community of faith?

_____

_____

_____

_____

_____

_____

_____

_____

_____

_____

_____

Activity 6:
Exploring Generosity

GENEROSITY

GOAL: Take a close look at your day-to-day expenditures.

> *I will bless those who bless you, and whoever curses you I will curse; and all peoples on earth will be blessed through you. —Genesis 12:11 (NIV)*

ACTION: The verse listed above is from Genesis, the very first book of the Bible. It establishes, right from the beginning, this chain reaction of blessings being paid forward. There are, of course, many ways to be a blessing. In this context the family of Abram (later Abraham) is going to be a witness to the God of the Universe for all the people groups of this world. You and I probably will start smaller.

One of the ways we are a blessing is that we share out of the resources God has provided us to make a difference in other people's lives. But we can't do that if we don't have any resources available because we have depleted them all. Sometimes we do this without even thinking about it. We spend several dollars on a fancy coffee at Starbucks when our homebrew would work just fine. We stop for fast food (which usually isn't very good for us) when we're just minutes from home.

Use a daily expense tracker to create an honest account of how you are spending your resources (find one you like by visiting an image search engine like www.images.google.com and typing in "daily expense tracker"). Start with a day to see just how quickly you notice patterns, then carry on for a week, keeping detailed notes.

JOURNAL REFLECTION: What did you discover about yourself and your spending habits? What are ways you could act differently, thus creating space for generosity?

_____

_____

_____

_____

EXPLORING

Part 3

Activity 1: Exploring Worship

 **WORSHIP**

 GOAL: Use the 5-finger prayer technique as a basis for prayer during worship.

> *Do not be anxious about anything, but in every situation, by prayer and petition, with thanksgiving, present your requests to God. And the peace of God, which transcends all understanding, will guard your hearts and your minds in Christ Jesus.*
> *—Philippians 4:6-7 (NIV)*

Using The Five Finger Prayer:

- **Thumb:** Pray for those closest to you (your family and friends).
- **Pointing finger:** Pray for those who teach, instruct, and heal, that they will receive support and wisdom in pointing others in the right direction (teachers, ministers, doctors).
- **Middle/tallest finger:** Pray for our leaders (the President, others in government leadership: local, state, national, leaders in business and industry, administrators).
- **Ring/weakest finger:** Pray for those who are sick, in trouble, underserved, and weak.
- **Pinky finger/the smallest finger of all:** Pray for yourself last, which is where we should place ourselves in relation to God and others...By the time you have prayed for the other four groups, your own needs will be put into proper perspective and you will be able to pray for yourself more effectively.

 **ACTION:** During the worship experience we not only offer our praise to God, but also seek God's blessing in our lives. The 5-finger prayer is a framework for remembering categories of people for whom we are called to pray. As you participate in worship this week, listen to the corporate prayer (sometimes offered as a pastoral prayer).

 JOURNAL REFLECTION: How were the categories of people acknowledged in the 5-finger prayer included in the prayer time(s) you experienced during corporate worship?

_____

_____

_____

_____

_____

Activity 2:
Exploring Hospitality

 HOSPITALITY

 GOAL: Observe the unique ways that followers of Christ love another.

> [Jesus speaking:] "A new command I give you; love one another. As I have loved you, so you must love one another. By this everyone will know that you are my disciples, if you love one another." —John 13:35 (NIV)

 **ACTION:** This verse from the Gospel of John suggests that followers of Christ will be uniquely recognizable by their love for one another. Try to identify at least five ways that you have observed Christians demonstrating love for one another (particularly in ways that set them apart as different from those who are not part of a faith community).

 JOURNAL REFLECTION: List the five ways you have observed (ideally, as specific examples you have seen in recent days, rather than generic examples).

_____

_____

_____

_____

_____

_____

_____

_____

_____

**Activity 3:
Exploring Being
Open to Jesus**

OPENING TO JESUS

 GOAL: Learn from a seasoned Christ-follower what it really means to follow Jesus.

> *After this, Jesus went out and saw a tax collector by the name of Levi sitting at his tax booth. "Follow me," Jesus said to him.* —Luke 5:27 (NIV)

 ACTION: In each of the Gospel accounts, Jesus extends an invitation: "Come, follow me." Have a conversation with a long-time believer about what it means to follow Jesus.

 JOURNAL REFLECTION: What insights did this conversation yield about what it means to follow Jesus? What surprised you? What challenged you about where you are in your own faith journey?

_____
_____
_____
_____
_____
_____
_____
_____
_____
_____

Activity 4:
Exploring Obedience

GOAL: Observe reminders of foundational principles of your faith.

> [Moses speaking:] "Hear, O Israel! The Lord is our God, the Lord is one! You shall love the Lord your God with all your heart and with all your soul and with all your might. These words, which I am commanding you today, shall be on your heart. You shall teach them diligently to your sons and shall talk of them when you sit in your house and when you walk by the way and when you lie down and when you rise up. You shall bind them as a sign on your hand and they shall be as frontals on your forehead. You shall write them on the doorposts of your house and on your gates." —Deuteronomy 6:4-9 (NIV)

ACTION: In this Old Testament passage (our Christian version of the ancient Hebrew Scriptures), we are reminded of the value of God's fundamental teachings as we strive to form our lives as pleasing to God. It is important to be surrounded by such reminders of what our priorities should be. In our homes, in our daily devotions, in our houses of worship, we should be constantly exposed to what we have written, literally and by our habits and disciplines, "on the doorposts of our houses and on our gates."

JOURNAL REFLECTION: In your own church (around the building, on your website, during worship) what reminders of the foundations of the faith are you exposed to? What visible reminders do you have around your home, in your car, on your person, or in the other places you regularly spend time?

_____

_____

_____

_____

_____

_____

Activity 5:
Exploring Service

 SERVICE

 GOAL: Explore the geographic possibilities for how your congregation encourages service.

> *[Jesus speaking:] "Whoever serves me must follow me; and where I am, my servant also will be. My Father will honor the one who serves me."* —John 12:26 (NIV)

 ACTION: In the previous week, we reviewed a copy of the church newsletter or scanned through the website for the church, thinking broadly about opportunities for service. This week, let's dig a little deeper to explore how this congregation is involved in serving others.

 JOURNAL REFLECTION: Write down specific ways in which this congregation offers opportunities to serve others.

• Locally _____
_____
_____

• Regionally _____
_____
_____

• Internationally _____
_____

Activity 6:
Exploring Generosity

 GENEROSITY

 GOAL: Diagnose yourself for symptoms of Affluenza.

Whoever loves money never has enough; whoever loves wealth is never satisfied with their income. This too is meaningless. —*Ecclesiastes 5:10 (NIV)*

 **ACTION:** Solomon, often described as one of the wisest men to have ever lived, wrote the words of that verse. Some students of our culture have noted that this is a lesson we still have not learned. They have even coined a term to describe our condition: Affluenza. This is the confluence of two words: affluence and influenza. It is suggested that we are infected with affluence, that we have a dysfunctional relationship with money. This is the result of three things prevalent in our culture: 1) materialism, 2) consumerism, and 3) easy debt.

 JOURNAL REFLECTION: Where do you see this disease at work in your life? Note specific personal observations for each of the three components of Affluenza.

_____

_____

_____

_____

_____

_____

_____

_____

_____

_____

EXPLORING

Part 4

Activity 1:
Exploring Worship

 WORSHIP

 **GOAL:** Consider the role of the offering in worship.

> *Honor the Lord with your wealth, with the first fruits of all your crops.*
> *—Proverbs 3:9 (NIV)*

 ACTION: As you attend the worship service this week, pay close attention to the time in the service where the "tithes and offerings" are collected. One of the ways we worship God is through the sharing of the resources God has provided to us to make a difference in the lives of those in our community and world. Usually there is some type of introduction to the 'offering' time where we are reminded about the difference our gifts are making in the world around us. This may be offered as a narrative, a video witness or often through the prayer that immediately precedes the offering.

 JOURNAL REFLECTION: How was the offering introduced in the worship service that you attended? Was there an emphasis on the ways in which congregational generosity impacts ministry, the local community, and the world? Was there a focus on which giving is a form of worship?

_____

_____

_____

_____

_____

_____

_____

Activity 2:
Exploring Hospitality

 HOSPITALITY

 GOAL: Share a meal with a friend and consider how the breaking of bread together enhances discipleship.

> *Every day they continued to meet together in the temple courts. They broke bread in their homes and ate together with glad and sincere hearts.* —Acts 2:46 (NIV)

 ACTION: Invite a friend to your home for dinner or meet at your favorite restaurant. The image of a shared meal is a common Scriptural image. For example, Jesus ate a meal as his last action with the disciples before the crucifixion. The image of a banquet where we share a meal is considered a precursor to the heavenly blessings.

 JOURNAL REFLECTION: Reflect on your experience:

What was it like to spend time together?

_____

_____

What did you talk about?

_____

_____

What did the experience show you about the depth of your friendship?

_____

_____

How was your experience a 'foretaste' of eternity?

_____

_____

Activity 3: Exploring Being Open to Jesus

OPENING TO JESUS

GOAL: Pay attention to the ways a sermon challenges you to open yourself to Jesus.

> *Examine yourselves to see whether you are in the faith; test yourselves. Do you not realize that Christ Jesus is in you—unless, of course, you fail the test?*
> *—2 Corinthians 13:5 (NIV)*

ACTION: A centerpiece of most corporate worship experiences is a teaching time, often referred to as the 'message' or 'sermon'. This teaching time is designed to help us engage the Scriptures as a guide to living life as God intends and experiencing the blessings God brings through that lifestyle. Each message or teaching time usually includes a specific invitation to take a next step in your discipleship journey.

JOURNAL REFLECTION: In the worship experience for this week, how were you invited to follow Jesus more fully? What specifically were you invited to do as one seeking to live life as God intends? How did these invitations connect to the Scripture lesson that was the focus of this worship service?

_____

_____

_____

_____

_____

_____

_____

_____

_____

_____

Activity 4:
Exploring Obedience

 OBEDIENCE

 GOAL: Use the practice of an Examen of Consciousness.

Rejoice in the Lord always. I will say it again: Rejoice! Let your gentleness be evident to all. The Lord is near. Do not be anxious about anything, but in every situation, by prayer and petition, with thanksgiving, present your requests to God. And the peace of God, which transcends all understanding, will guard your hearts and your minds in Christ Jesus. —Philippians 4:4-7 (NIV)

 ACTION: This is an amazing promise. The Lord is near. An Examen of Consciousness (sometimes also referred to as Examen of Conscience), is a practice of disciples of Jesus throughout the ages to help develop an awareness of the presence of God in our lives. It is really very simple:

- Find yourself a quiet space.
- Close your eyes and imagine rolling a recording of your day backwards.
- Note the situations and encounters you have been part of during the day.
- Consider where God might have been at work—either with your awareness or without.

This might include the joy of being with those you love; or being given just the right words to say in a difficult situation; or a sense of forgiveness when you made a mistake.

 JOURNAL REFLECTION: Did you find this exercise helpful? What insights were revealed to you? How was this technique different from your normal spiritual reflections?

_____

_____

_____

_____

Activity 5:
Exploring Service

GOAL: Acknowledge the specific ways God has gifted you for service.

For we are God's handiwork, created in Christ Jesus to do good works, which God prepared in advance for us to do. –Ephesians 2:10 (NIV)

ACTION: All of us, according to Scripture, have been given abilities by God so that we can be used by God to do good works. We refer to these abilities as talents or strengths.

What talents or strengths has God placed in you? After following the response prompt below, review your list and give thanks to God for each thing listed. Meditate briefly about how each of these is being used already or might be used in the future to honor God.

JOURNAL REFLECTION: Write down 10 separate things that you do well.

_____

_____

_____

_____

_____

_____

_____

_____

_____

_____

Activity 6:
Exploring Generosity

 **GENEROSITY**

 GOAL: Consider the dangers of debt.

The rich rule over the poor, and the borrower is slave to the lender.
—Proverbs 22:7 (NIV)

 **ACTION:** We live in a world of easy access to credit cards which give us tempting access to money that we may not have readily available. This is both a blessing and a curse. Count the number of credit card offers you receive during any given week. It is not unusual to receive several. Easy money. Easy debt.

 **JOURNAL REFLECTION:** How have you experienced or directly observed the borrower being slave to the lender? Be as specific as possible. What are the ramifications of such indebtedness?

_____

_____

_____

_____

_____

_____

_____

_____

_____

_____

EXPLORING

Part 5

Activity 1:
Exploring Worship

WORSHIP

GOAL: Consider more deeply the role of singing in worship.

I will declare your name to my brothers and sisters; in the assembly I will sing your praises." —Hebrews 2:12 (NIV)

ACTION: An important part of the worship experience is the singing of praise songs or hymns (depending on the style of worship). John Wesley, the founder of the Methodist Church, gave these instructions for singing in worship to the Methodists:

• Sing them exactly as they are printed.
• Sing all. See that you join with the congregation as frequently as you can.
• Sing lustily and with good courage.
• Sing modestly.
• Above all sing spiritually.

(United Methodist Hymnal p. vii)

Wesley wanted people to sing songs as they were printed because the songs were more than just music or even praise. Songs teach us about God and about ourselves and about our relationship with God. As you participate in worship this week, consider the words to one of the songs that is sung.

JOURNAL REFLECTION: What was the song on which you chose to focus? What did the words of that song teach you about who God is? How did they inspire or instruct you? What was the difference between singing the words together with others and contemplating them alone?

_____

_____

_____

_____

_____

Activity 2:
Exploring Hospitality

HOSPITALITY

GOAL: Make room for others by living out the 'one anothers'.

The Epistles (letters in the last part of the New Testament) are full of admonitions called the 'one anothers'. Here are just a few:

- Be devoted to one another. —Romans 12:10 (NIV)
- Live in harmony with one another. —Romans 12:16 (NIV)
- Accept one another. —Romans 15:17 (NIV)
- Have equal concern for each other. —1 Corinthians 12:25 (NIV)
- Serve one another. —Galatians 5:13 (NIV)

ACTION: Henry Nouwen, a Catholic priest and prolific author, writes that hospitality is about "making room" for someone in our lives. He notes that the person does not have to be someone we would usually relate to or someone who lives the same lifestyle that we do. In fact, Nouwen encourages us to get to know people outside of our normal circle—to hear their stories and to share ours, to engage them in a way that expresses acceptance and value.

JOURNAL REFLECTION: How have you "made room" for someone in your life this week by practicing the 'one anothers'? Be as specific as possible.

_____

_____

_____

_____

_____

_____

Activity 3: Exploring Being Open to Jesus

 OPENING TO JESUS

 GOAL: Use the Lord's Prayer as a guide for living as a committed disciple.

> [Jesus speaking:] "This, then, is how you should pray:
> Our Father, who art in heaven,
> Hallowed be thy name.
> Thy kingdom come, thy will be done
> On earth as it is in heaven.
> Give us this day our daily bread
> And forgive us our trespasses
> As we forgive those who trespass against us.
> And lead us not into temptation
> But deliver us from evil,
> For thine is the Kingdom, and the power, and the glory forever. Amen.
> —Matthew 6:9-13 (NIV)

 ACTION: Disciples from the earliest days have used this prayer as part of their devotional life. It is the prayer Jesus taught the original 12 disciples to pray.

 JOURNAL REFLECTION: What specific guidance does this prayer give us for how disciples are to live? How do you feel you could grow in each of these areas?

_____

_____

_____

_____

_____

_____

Activity 4:
Exploring Obedience

 OBEDIENCE

 GOAL: Move beyond an obsession with rules to a deeper understanding of God's desires.

> *Since you died with Christ to the elemental spiritual forces of this world, why, as though you still belonged to the world, do you submit to its rules: "Do not handle! Do not taste! Do not touch!"? These rules, which have to do with things that are all destined to perish with use, are based on merely human commands and teachings. Such regulations indeed have an appearance of wisdom, with their self-imposed worship, their false humility and their harsh treatment of the body, but they lack any value in restraining sensual indulgence.* —Colossians 2:20-23 (NIV)

 **ACTION:** Some of us grew up with a little ditty that goes like this:

Don't dance,
Don't drink,
Don't smoke,
Don't chew.
And don't hang around
With those who do.

It could seem like discipleship is focused on the rules about all the things we aren't supposed to do. And all the punishment to be received for doing all the things we aren't supposed to do. But true discipleship moves beyond this simple understanding of prohibitions to a deeper appreciation of the freedom granted us in Christ and how best to use it.

 JOURNAL REFLECTION: What rules have you perceived as being most important to church folk? What particular rules or prohibitions have caused you or others to struggle? Which rules for living do you consider most important?

_____

_____

_____

_____

Activity 5:
Exploring Service

 | **SERVICE**

GOAL: Ask people why they serve.

> *Be devoted to one another in love. Honor one another above yourselves.*
> *—Romans 12:10 (NIV)*

ACTION: The Scriptures frequently encourage us to "serve one another." Having paid close attention to the many ways to serve within your local congregation, do an interview with two or three people who you know serve in some capacity at your church. Ask them why they serve and how that service affects them. Ask them what is most difficult about serving and what is most rewarding. Why would they encourage other people to serve?

JOURNAL REFLECTION: Summarize the response to your interviews below. What insights did you gain from these conversations? Were there any surprises? Did you hear anything you hadn't expected to hear? Was anything unsaid that you expected to hear? How did these conversations make you think about your own attitudes towards service?

_____

_____

_____

_____

_____

_____

_____

_____

_____

_____

Activity 6:
Exploring Generosity

 GENEROSITY

 GOAL: Approach God from a posture of dependence.

> [Jesus speaking:] "Give us this day our daily bread". —Matthew 6:11 (NIV)

 ACTION: Today's focus verse is one of the verses we read earlier in the section that make up the Lord's Prayer. The kind of specific request stated in this verse is a type of prayer known as a petition, which means we are actively asking God for something. This particular request, of course, is not just about bread to eat but about asking God more generally to provide for our daily needs. It is about living in a posture of dependence on God.

 JOURNAL REFLECTION: How are you depending on God to meet your needs? How has God provided for you in the past?

_____
_____
_____
_____
_____
_____
_____
_____
_____
_____

EXPLORING

Part 6

Activity 1: Exploring Worship

 **WORSHIP**

 GOAL: Observe the ways in which worship through service is encouraged.

> [L]et us continually offer to God a sacrifice of praise—the fruit of lips that openly profess his name. And do not forget to do good and to share with others, for with such sacrifices God is pleased. —Hebrews 13:15-16 (NIV)

 ACTION: This text from Hebrews reminds us that worship is bigger than singing songs and praying prayers. Worship includes the continual offering of our lives to God (doing good and sharing with others). As you participate in congregational worship this week at your local church, pay attention to how the serving of others is witnessed to and celebrated. Are stories of service shared as part of the worship service? Do you see printed or projected images of service? Do you hear directly from people who have been serving God by serving others? Are you challenged to serve in the week ahead?

 JOURNAL REFLECTION: Write down the ways in which you observed references to serving others during the worship service you attended. In what ways did you see evidence of people living lives of service, even if this service was not overtly mentioned? What inspired or challenged you about what you saw or heard? Were any obvious opportunities missed?

_____

_____

_____

_____

_____

_____

_____

_____

Activity 2:
Exploring Hospitality

HOSPITALITY

GOAL: Pray for someone who needs a blessing from God.

> I urge, then, first of all, that petitions, prayers, **intercession** and thanksgiving be made for all people. —Timothy 2:1 (NIV)

ACTION: These words were written by Paul to his young friend and protégé, Timothy. Intercession is the act of seeking God's blessing or direct aid (intercession) in the life of another person. It is a form of prayer where we seek to be a blessing to others. Visualize someone in your life who could definitely use a blessing from God. As a form of praying, hold your hands together, palms up, and visualize lifting this person up into the presence of God.

JOURNAL REFLECTION: Write down the names of three additional people whose current situations could benefit from a Godly intervention.

1. _____

2. _____

3. _____

Lift them up in the manner suggested above, and for a real bonus, let them know you did. What was it like to pray for them? What thoughts and feelings passed through your mind during and after this time of prayer? How would this type of prayer affect the way you extend yourself to them?

_____

_____

_____

_____

_____

Activity 3: Exploring Being Open to Jesus

OPENING TO JESUS

GOAL: Make note of what it means to be blessed by the people of God.

> *"I will make you into a great nation, and I will bless you;*
> *I will make your name great, and you will be a blessing.*
> *I will bless those who bless you, and whoever curses you I will curse;*
> *and all peoples on earth   will be blessed through you."*
> —*Genesis 12:2-3 (NIV)*

ACTION: When God first called Abram (commonly known by his later name, Abraham) to be the founder of God's people, God made this promise, found in Genesis, chapter 12. The long arc of God's grace as recorded history in the Bible is the story of this great nation and how it did, indeed, bless all the peoples of the Earth. It is a reminder, for those of us whose adoption into the family of God has been made possible by the sacrifice of Jesus Christ, of just how blessed we have been by our Godly family, and how we are called to likewise bless others.

JOURNAL REFLECTION: How have you experienced being blessed by the people of God? Make a list of at least 10 ways you have been directly blessed by the body of believers.

_____

_____

_____

_____

_____

_____

_____

_____

Activity 4: Exploring Obedience

 OBEDIENCE

 GOAL: Consider the meaning of the eternal life promised by Jesus.

> [Jesus speaking:] "Very truly I tell you, whoever hears my word and believes him who sent me has **eternal life** and will not be judged but has crossed over from death to life". —John 5:24 (NIV)

 ACTION: One of the amazing gifts from God is that those who believe in Jesus (commit themselves to becoming like Jesus) experience a newness of life. This is often called 'eternal life' or 'abundant life' or 'wholeness' or 'wellness'. Too often, eternal life is only talked about in terms of what happens after death (physical death). But note in the above verse from the Gospel of John that eternal life is described by Jesus in the <u>present</u> tense—"whoever hears my word . . . <u>has</u> eternal life."

 **JOURNAL REFLECTION:** How might God help you have 'eternal life' or 'abundant life' right now? What wholeness are you seeking?

_____

_____

_____

_____

_____

_____

_____

_____

_____

_____

Activity 5: Exploring Service

GOAL: Help someone in a simple, straightforward way.

> [N]ot looking to your own interests but each of you to the interests of the others.
> —Philippians 2:4 (NIV)

ACTION: Take time this week to help someone other than a neighbor. It can be a friend or co-worker, or, even better, a total stranger. It could be as simple as watching their children, giving them a ride, running an errand, or cleaning up after them. Service to others doesn't have to be a big program. In fact, it is most biblically a lifestyle.

JOURNAL REFLECTION: How did you serve? What did it feel like to support someone? How was being available for this service an inconvenience to you? Why was it worth it?

_____

_____

_____

_____

_____

_____

_____

_____

_____

_____

_____

Activity 6:
Exploring Generosity

 GENEROSITY

 GOAL: Be generous in a way other than giving money.

A generous person will prosper; whoever refreshes others will be refreshed.
—Proverbs 11:25 (NIV)

 ACTION: Most of the time when we think about the theme of generosity, the image of money comes to mind. We think of it in terms of being generous with our financial resources. But generosity is bigger than that. We can also be generous with our time and our knowledge and our skills. For example, taking an hour to help a child learn how to read is an act of generosity with far-reaching, life-changing impact. Helping a neighbor with a building project is an act of generosity, too. These kinds of generosity build relationships and can lead to powerful connections.

Find a way this week to be generous in a way other than giving money.

 **JOURNAL REFLECTION:** What opportunity for generosity did you embrace? Write down the details. How did it feel to be a 'generous' person? What results can you see this kind of generosity having that are different from just giving someone (or some worthy project) money?

_____

_____

_____

_____

_____

_____

_____

_____

_____

BEGINNING

Part 1

Activity 1:
Beginning Worship

WORSHIP

GOAL: Establish a dedicated time and place for spending quality time with God.

> *Very early in the morning, while it was still dark, Jesus got up, left the house and went off to a solitary place, where he prayed. Simon and his companions went to look for him, and when they found him, they exclaimed: "Everyone is looking for you!"* —Mark 1:35-37 (NIV)

ACTION: As seen in this passage from the Gospel of Mark, Jesus models for us the importance of having a time and space of quiet to spend with God. Decide on a time and place where you and God can spend some time together each day. It could be a closet like in *War Room*, the recent popular movie with a literal prayer closet, or it could be just a favorite easy chair and a time where you will have no distractions. You are encouraged to spend time each day in prayer and Bible reading. You may want to start slowly with just 5-10 minutes.

JOURNAL REFLECTION: What are some of the places you considered for your time-with-God place? What did you decide on for this activity action? What are the particular challenges of having a designated place and time for getting closer to God? Come back here after a few days and write down your experiences.

_____
_____
_____
_____
_____
_____

Activity 2:
Beginning Hospitality

 HOSPITALITY

 GOAL: Consider how engagement with others leads to spiritual growth.

> [Jesus speaking:] *"My prayer is not for them alone. I pray also for those who will believe in me through their message, that all of them may be one, Father, just as you are in me and I am in you. May they also be in us so that the world may believe that you have sent me. I have given them the glory that you gave me, that they may be one as we are one—I in them and you in me—so that they may be brought to complete unity. Then the world will know that you sent me and have loved them even as you have loved me."*
> —John 17:20-23 (NIV)

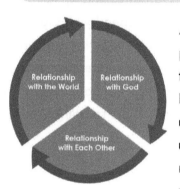

ACTION: In the Scripture verses above, circle the words or phrases that catch your attention. You may have noticed that there is a pattern reflected in these verses. As we ("those who believe") become one with God ("be in us") we are brought to unity ("one as we are one") with other believers, and through us the world may believe. In other words, as we grow in our relationship with God, we are led into a deeper relationship with each other. As we grow in relationship with each other, our witness in the world grows stronger. As our witness in the world grows stronger, our faith grows deeper. And the process continues.

 JOURNAL REFLECTION: How do you see your faith growing as you engage other believers and even those beyond the church? Give specific examples. Can such growth happen absent of engagement? How is choosing to engage others a unique growth strategy?

_____

_____

_____

_____

_____

Activity 3:
Beginning
Being Open to Jesus

OPENING TO JESUS

GOAL: Use the ACTS model to guide your prayer.

And pray in the Spirit on all occasions with all kinds of prayers and requests. With this in mind, be alert and always keep on praying for all the Lord's people.
—Ephesians 6:18 (NIV)

The ACTS Model for Getting Started with Prayer:

One of the simplest and most well-known models for a prayer time is the ACTS format:

A – **Adoration:** Proclaiming who God is and the attributes of His character

C – **Confession/Proclamation:** Personal cleansing, repentance, putting on of Christ's nature

T – **Thanksgiving:** Praise offering, remembering the works of the Lord, meditation

S – **Supplication:** Asking, intercession, and petitioning according to His will

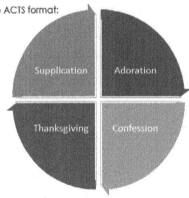

ACTION: As you spend your quiet time with God (see Activity 1), practice praying using the ACTS Model described above.

JOURNAL REFLECTION: How did you express adoration for God? What were you led to confess? What were you thankful for? Who did you pray for? Did you find this an effective guide for your prayer time?

_____

_____

_____

_____

_____

Activity 4:
Beginning Obedience

OBEDIENCE

GOAL: Consider the mystery of our redemption from sin through Jesus.

> [F]or all have sinned and fall short of the glory of God, and all are justified freely by his grace through the redemption that came by Christ Jesus. God presented Christ as a sacrifice of atonement, through the shedding of his blood—to be received by faith. He did this to demonstrate his righteousness, because in his forbearance he had left the sins committed beforehand unpunished. —Romans 3:23-25 (NIV)

ACTION: These are deep theological concepts: justification, grace, redemption, atonement, righteousness. Read this passage again, this time as interpreted by Eugene Peterson in *The Message*, and see if a different rendering helps you understand these concepts more fully.

Since we've compiled this long and sorry record as sinners (both us and them) and proved that we are utterly incapable of living the glorious lives God wills for us, God did it for us. Out of sheer generosity he put us in right standing with himself. A pure gift. He got us out of the mess we're in and restored us to where he always wanted us to be. And he did it by means of Jesus Christ. —Romans 3:23-25 (The Message)

JOURNAL REFLECTION: What do these verses tell you about God? What do these verses tell you about humankind (you)? What do these verses reveal about our relationship with God?

_____

_____

_____

_____

_____

_____

_____

Activity 5:
Beginning Service

SERVICE

GOAL: Choose a way to serve within your local congregation.

You, my brothers and sisters, were called to be free. But do not use your freedom to indulge the flesh; rather, serve one another humbly in love. —Galatians 5:13 (NIV)

ACTION: Explore ways that you could serve in the congregation where you are worshiping. Perhaps you could help set up for a meeting, clean up after an event, answer phones in the office, fold bulletins, or mail correspondence. There are endless needs in most congregations where you can find ways to serve. If possible, serve alongside others so that you get to know more people. It is quite likely you are already serving in some capacity. If so, you may reflect on that existing service, but even better, find some small way to have a fresh experience of service.

JOURNAL REFLECTION: How did you serve? What did it feel like to serve your church? Who did you get to know or know better in the process? How did this service require humility?

_____

_____

_____

_____

_____

_____

_____

_____

_____

_____

_____

Activity 6:
Beginning Generosity

GOAL: Consider the deeper motivations behind your acts of generosity.

[Jesus speaking:] "Be careful not to practice your righteousness in front of others to be seen by them. If you do, you will have no reward from your Father in heaven. So when you give to the needy, do not announce it with trumpets, as the hypocrites do in the synagogues and on the streets, to be honored by others. Truly I tell you, they have received their reward in full. But when you give to the needy, do not let your left hand know what your right hand is doing, so that your giving may be in secret. Then your Father, who sees what is done in secret, will reward you". —Matthew 6:1-4 (NIV)

ACTION: The reality is that even in Jesus' day, no one actually announced their gifts to the needy with trumpets or made a show of distributing gifts on the streets. But people then, as with people now, did occasionally seek recognition for what they had done. Jesus called them hypocrites (actors on a stage) and said they had already received their reward. What Jesus was pointing out was the motivation for what was being done. When we call attention to our generosity, an unhealthy part of our motivation is about being recognized. Jesus calls us to be motivated solely by our love for God who brings the amazing love to us in the first place.

JOURNAL REFLECTION: Think about the ways you have supported the work of the church through your generosity. Have you ever felt underappreciated or unrecognized? Give specific examples. Have you been generous anonymously? How is this a different experience from people knowing about the gifts you have made?

_____

_____

_____

_____

_____

_____

BEGINNING

∿ ∿ ∿ ∿ ∿

Part 2

Activity 1:
Beginning Worship

WORSHIP

GOAL: Experience the role of providing hospitality in a worship setting.

Share with the Lord's people who are in need. Practice hospitality. —Romans 12:13 (NIV)

ACTION: Volunteer to serve with the Hospitality Team (or as an usher or greeter) for a worship service where you attend church.

JOURNAL REFLECTION: How does this team support a sense of worshipfulness? How do people respond to the hospitality extended? Who did you meet? What did it feel like to support your church?

_____

_____

_____

_____

_____

_____

_____

_____

_____

_____

Activity 2: Beginning Hospitality

 HOSPITALITY

 GOAL: Strike up a conversation and see what happens.

> *But it is you, a man like myself, my companion, my close friend, with whom I once enjoyed sweet fellowship at the house of God, as we walked about among the worshipers.*
> *—Psalm 55:13-14 (NIV)*

 ACTION: Meet someone new or connect with someone you don't know very well. Arrange a time to have a conversation where the focus is on getting to know them or know them better. You might consider questions like:

- Tell me a little about your family.
- Where did you grow up? How did you end up here?
- What do you do besides go to church?

 JOURNAL REFLECTION: What was it like to connect with someone at a deeper level than a superficial greeting? How might this conversation change the way you interact in the future?

_____

_____

_____

_____

_____

_____

_____

_____

Activity 3:
Beginning
Being Open to Jesus

OPENING TO JESUS

GOAL: Use a daily devotion to guide your quiet time with God.

Early the next morning they arose and worshiped before the Lord and then went back to their home at Ramah. —1 Samuel 1:19 (NIV)

ACTION: One of the foundations of the spiritual life is having a daily time focused on your relationship with God. Last week you read about Jesus taking time apart to be with the Father. A great tool for framing this time with God is a daily devotional guide. Many churches offer this resource or you can find them online (e.g. www.upperroom.org). Pick up a guide or subscribe online and try this practice of spending time with God each day.

JOURNAL REFLECTION: How is this helpful for you? What gets in the way of this time with God? How can you make this a priority?

_____

_____

_____

_____

_____

_____

_____

_____

Activity 4:
Beginning Obedience

 OBEDIENCE

 GOAL: Consider the manner in which a person may make a profession of faith.

If you declare with your mouth, "Jesus is Lord," and believe in your heart that God raised him from the dead, you will be saved. –Romans 10:9 (NIV)

 **ACTION:** A starting point in the journey as a disciple of Jesus Christ is the act of making a profession of faith and inviting Jesus to be your Lord and Savior. Different Christian traditions have a variety of ways that this is accomplished. Have a conversation this week with a maturing disciple or your pastor about what is recommended in your tradition.

 **JOURNAL REFLECTION:** What did you learn? How did you respond?

_____

_____
_____
_____
_____
_____
_____
_____
_____
_____
_____
_____

Activity 5:
Beginning Service

SERVICE

GOAL: Ask someone else about your gifts and talents.

There are different kinds of gifts, but the same Spirit distributes them. There are different kinds of service, but the same Lord. There are different kinds of working, but in all of them and in everyone it is the same God at work. —1 Corinthians 12:4-6 (NIV)

ACTION: The Scripture passage above reinforces the fundamental idea that all disciples are uniquely gifted by God for service within the "body of Christ." We often refer to the unique ways in which we are gifted as talents or abilities, and in an earlier activity we had you list your own perceived talents. Now it's time to see what others think. Ask a couple of different people (one who knows you very well and one who has worked with you but knows you less well personally) and write down five things that they identify as talents or abilities that you possess.

JOURNAL REFLECTION: Did the talents and abilities they noted align with what you had observed about yourself? Were there any surprises or new insights? How does it make you feel to know that other people think you're good at the same things you think you're good at? How did it make you feel to be noticed for things you did not think of as strengths that you possessed?

_____

_____

_____

_____

_____

_____

_____

_____

Activity 6:
Beginning Generosity

 **GENEROSITY**

 GOAL: Consider what it means to be a cheerful giver.

Each of you should give what you have decided in your heart to give, not reluctantly or under compulsion, for God loves a cheerful giver. —2 Corinthians 9:7 (NIV)

 ACTION: Richard Foster, spiritual guide and author of many great resources, states that often the last part of our lives to be converted (offered to God) is our wallet or pocketbook. According to Paul, giving is is not something we do to meet a religious law or obligation. It is a way we can participate in the work God is doing through the Church. Paul encourages us to be cheerful givers.

 JOURNAL REFLECTION: What encourages cheerful giving? How has this been part of your spiritual practice? What discourages you from cheerful giving? What makes you a grumpy, skeptical, or recalcitrant giver?

_____

_____

_____

_____

_____

_____

_____

_____

_____

_____

_____

BEGINNING

~ ~ ~ ~ ~

Part 3

Activity 1: Beginning Worship

WORSHIP

GOAL: Consider the ways you can connect your personal devotions with corporate worship.

> *The Lord says: "These people come near to me with their mouth and honor me with their lips, but their hearts are far from me. Their worship of me is based on merely human rules they have been taught.* —Isaiah 29:13 (NIV)

ACTION: As you participate in corporate worship this week, note how prayer and Scripture reading are encouraged. For example, are you encouraged to pray for those on a prayer list? Is there a special need in the community? Is reference made to prayer as part of your daily devotional time? Are you encouraged to read and reflect on a particular Scripture prior to worship the next week? Are you provided with a devotional reading? A list of Scriptures for devotional time?

JOURNAL REFLECTION: What does this tell you about the priority of prayer and biblical reflection for this community of faith?

_____

_____

_____

_____

_____

_____

_____

_____

_____

Activity 2: Beginning Hospitality

 HOSPITALITY

 GOAL: Consider the call to forgiveness, essential to discipleship.

> [Jesus speaking:] "And forgive us our debts, as we also have forgiven our debtors".
> —Matthew 6:12 (NIV)

 **ACTION:** Pray the Lord's Prayer again (found in Matthew 6). As you consider the petition "forgive us for our trespasses as we forgive those who trespass against us," take time to reflect carefully on your own life. Forgiveness is not the same as forgetting about something. It does not dismiss the act as irrelevant. Forgiveness is choosing not to hold something against someone. It is a decision not to let some action destroy the relationship.

 JOURNAL REFLECTION: Who has wronged you in some way that you might need to forgive? What have you done that you might need to seek forgiveness for? Be specific.

_____
_____
_____
_____
_____
_____
_____
_____
_____

Activity 3:
Beginning
Being Open to Jesus

OPENING TO JESUS

GOAL: Let go of the world, and make yourself available to Jesus.

Do not conform to the pattern of this world, but be transformed by the renewing of your mind. Then you will be able to test and approve what God's will is—his good, pleasing and perfect will. —Romans 12:2 (NIV)

ACTION: Read and reflect on the following verses from ...a poem titled, "Guerrillas of Grace," by Ted Loder:

...O God, let something essential and joyful happen in me now,
something like the blooming of hope and faith,
like a grateful heart, like a surge of awareness
of how precious each moment is....

JOURNAL REFLECTION: What did this prayer communicate to you? How did you feel as you read and meditated upon these words?

_____

_____
_____
_____
_____
_____
_____
_____
_____
_____
_____

Activity 4:
Beginning Obedience

OBEDIENCE

GOAL: Live life as a continual offering to God.

But you are a chosen people, a royal priesthood, a holy nation, God's special possession, that you may declare the praises of him who called you out of darkness into his wonderful light. Once you were not a people, but now you are the people of God; once you had not received mercy, but now you have received mercy. Dear friends, I urge you, as foreigners and exiles, to abstain from sinful desires, which wage war against your soul. Live such good lives among the pagans that, though they accuse you of doing wrong, they may see your good deeds and glorify God on the day he visits us.
—1 Peter 2:9-12 (NIV)

ACTION: Discipleship, as described here by Peter, is not a part-time gig. It's not a buffet selection of options of when to serve God and when not to serve God. It is a 24/7 commitment to living for God at all times and in all situations. There are no exemptions, secret spaces, or vacations. We are called to holy work.

JOURNAL REFLECTION: What would our lives look like if we took Peter's words seriously? If we thought of ourselves as "chosen by God for priestly work" (rather than leaving this work to professional clergy)? How would serious consideration of our responsibility to honor this work change our behaviors, our priorities, our relationships?

_____

_____

_____

_____

_____

_____

_____

_____

Activity 5:
Beginning Service

SERVICE

GOAL: Take a closer look at your spiritual gifts.

> *Now to each one the manifestation of the Spirit is given for the common good.... All these are the work of one and the same Spirit, and he distributes them to each one, just as he determines.* —1 Corinthians 12:7 and 12:11 (NIV)

ACTION: Last week you read the Scripture selection from 1 Corinthians 12: 1-27 where the Apostle Paul described the body of Christ in terms of each person being given certain gifts to do the Kingdom work. Take a spiritual gifts inventory. You can find a free one by using an online search engine and entering the phrase, "spiritual gifts assessment United Methodist Church."

JOURNAL REFLECTION: What were your top three gifts? What does that tell you about how God might use you in serving others?

_____

_____

_____

_____

_____

_____

_____

_____

_____

_____

Activity 6:
Beginning Generosity

 **GENEROSITY**

 GOAL: Learn to be content with what you already have.

> *I am not saying this because I am in need, for I have learned to be content whatever the circumstances. I know what it is to be in need, and I know what it is to have plenty. I have learned the secret of being content in any and every situation, whether well fed or hungry, whether living in plenty or in want. I can do all this through him who gives me strength. —Philippians 4:11-13 (NIV)*

 ACTION: In a previous activity we explored the "disease" of Affluenza. In this activity, thinking more deeply about Paul's comments on contentment, take a closer look at your own relationship with material possessions. Write down a couple of examples of the worst purchases you ever made (things you couldn't afford or were obsessed with obtaining then disappointed by, decisions you later regretted, etc.). Conversely you might record a couple of instances in which you thought about making a purchase but decided to wait or abandon that acquisition altogether.

 JOURNAL REFLECTION: What would it mean for you to be content with what God has already provided? What would be the benefit?

_____

_____

_____

_____

_____

_____

_____

_____

_____

BEGINING

Part 4

Activity 1:
Beginning Worship

 WORSHIP

 GOAL: Pay attention to your gut response when challenged to serve.`

> *For what we preach is not ourselves, but Jesus Christ as Lord, and ourselves as your servants for Jesus' sake. —2 Corinthians 4:5 (NIV)*

 ACTION: As you participate in corporate worship this week, pay attention to the ways in which you are invited to serve. This exercise is focused on thinking about the ways you are publicly invited to serve and how you internally respond to such appeals. Perhaps it is to set up or clean up for a church activity. It could be a community service project. Your congregation may be sending a mission team to serve the underprivileged or in disaster response. You might be encouraged to see the needs right around you in your neighborhood and find a way to respond.

 JOURNAL REFLECTION: How were you challenged to serve (respond in an active way) during the worship service? How did you respond? A selfless response to such calls to action are an inextricable part of a lifestyle of worship. Did you immediately have a reflexive response (negative or positive)? What do you think was behind that ? Could you see signs of response (enthusiastic or wary) in the people around you?

_____

_____

_____

_____

_____

_____

_____

Activity 2:
Beginning Hospitality

GOAL: Get to know someone different from you a little bit better.

There is neither Jew nor Gentile, neither slave nor free, nor is there male and female, for you are all one in Christ Jesus. —Galatians 3:28 (NIV)

ACTION: In the place where you work, or play, or even worship, it is likely that there are people who are different than you or live a different lifestyle than yours. The prayer model Jesus gave his disciples with "Our Father…" is a clear witness that we are all children of the same God. Or as Paul puts it in Galatians 3:28, "We are all one in Christ Jesus." Look for an opportunity this week to have a conversation with someone who is different from you (ethnically, culturally, linguistically, or by virtue of the lifestyle they have chosen).

JOURNAL REFLECTION: What did you learn about them? What did you learn from this experience? How do you think things might be changed if you regularly sought out these kinds of conversations and connections?

Activity 3:
Beginning
Being Open to Jesus

OPENING TO JESUS

GOAL: Insert yourself actively into the world, and pray for what you see.

> *And pray in the Spirit on all occasions with all kinds of prayers and requests. With this in mind, be alert and always keep on praying for all the Lord's people.*
> *—Ephesians 6:18 (NIV)*

ACTION: We most often associate prayer with finding a quiet place and closing our eyes and having a conversation with God. But prayer can also be experienced by walking around and paying attention to what God sees. This week take a walk around your neighborhood or around your workplace and focus on seeing that community as God sees it. When given an insight, take time to pray. Particularly, pray for the people you see along the way.

JOURNAL REFLECTION: What caught your attention? How were you encouraged to pray for the needs in your community? What people did you take time to pray for that you might not have prayed for otherwise?

_____

_____

_____

_____

_____

_____

_____

_____

_____

_____

Activity 4:
Beginning Obedience

 OBEDIENCE

GOAL: Consider the difference between talk and action.

Dear children, let us not love with words or speech but with actions and in truth. This is how we know that we belong to the truth and how we set our hearts at rest in his presence: If our hearts condemn us, we know that God is greater than our hearts, and he knows everything. —1 John 3:18-20 (NIV)

ACTION: John's letter is all about the ways in which "love is a verb." One of the main complaints non-Christians have about followers of Jesus is that those followers are too often guilty of hypocrisy: teaching or preaching the gospel of love and not following through in practice. The Bible is clear that our deeds are more important than our words. Reading through the accounts of Jesus' life, as recorded by the disciples, we can observe the way in which Jesus (literally) practiced what he preached.

JOURNAL REFLECTION: Write down at least five examples of statements Jesus made about loving others and corresponding examples in which he showed that very love. How would you evaluate your own efforts to practice what you preach? Be specific (and be honest with yourself).

_____

_____

_____

_____

_____

_____

_____

_____

_____

Activity 5: Beginning Service

 SERVICE

 GOAL: Identify your passions for service in particular areas and with particular groups.

> *Never be lacking in zeal, but keep your spiritual fervor, serving the Lord.*
> *—Romans 12:11 (NIV)*

 ACTION: Consider the following list. Where do you sense passion for making a difference?

- Children
- Youth
- Discipleship
- Poverty
- Elderly
- Hungry
- Homeless
- Education
- Finances
- Single Parents
- Medically Needy
- Special Needs Families
- Terminally Ill
- Those Experiencing Grief
- Social Justice

 JOURNAL REFLECTION: How might you be called to serve in these areas or others you can think of?

_____

_____

_____

_____

_____

_____

_____

_____

_____

Activity 6:
Beginning Generosity

GENEROSITY

GOAL: Review your own practice of regular giving to the church.

> *Joash said to the priests, "Collect all the money that is brought as sacred offerings to the temple of the Lord—the money collected in the census, the money received from personal vows and the money brought voluntarily to the temple." —2 Kings 12:4 (NIV)*

ACTION: When we give to the church, it is a way of supporting the ministries and mission of that community of faith. Regular giving is a spiritual practice that encourages us to put the needs of others above our own wants and desires. It is a way of worshiping God as we share a portion of what God has provided to help others.

You are encouraged to consider making giving a regular practice. The amount is not particularly important. It is the act of giving.

JOURNAL REFLECTION: If you are not already giving as a regular practice, what amount could you commit to give on a weekly basis? If you are, reflect on what you are currently giving. How would you describe your experience to others? When did you first decide to give in this way, and how has that giving evolved over time?

_____

_____

_____

_____

_____

_____

_____

_____

BEGINNING

Part 5

Activity 1:
Beginning Worship

WORSHIP

GOAL: Worship God in your moment-by-moment treatment of others.

> *Whoever claims to love God yet hates a brother or sister is a liar. For whoever does not love their brother and sister, whom they have seen, cannot love God, whom they have not seen. And he has given us this command: Anyone who loves God must also love their brother and sister. —1 John 4:20-21 (NIV)*

ACTION: We tend to associate the idea of worship with the gathering together of believers to engage in the corporate acts of praise, prayer, proclamation (teaching), and presence (sacraments). But worship is bigger than the corporate activities. Worship is a personal lifestyle. Worship is about bringing honor and glory to God in everything we do as we live our lives. For example, the way we use our financial resources is an opportunity to worship; so is the way treat our neighbors; so is the way we engage family, co-workers, friends, and even store clerks in relationship.

JOURNAL REFLECTION: Consider recent encounters with friends, co-workers, and family members. Can you think of a specific interaction in which your actions and words brought honor to God? Can you think of a specific interaction in which your actions and words did not?

_____

_____

_____

_____

_____

_____

_____

_____

Activity 2:
Beginning Hospitality

HOSPITALITY

GOAL: Explore the idea of a spiritual friend.

> A friend loves at all times, and a brother is born for a time of adversity.
> —Proverbs 17:17 (NIV)

ACTION: Relationships are important. We are designed to live in community. In fact, we become our best selves through supporting, encouraging, and empowering "one another" (as first explored in an earlier activity on hospitality). Check out the infographic at www.overviewbible.com (type 'one another' in the search box) and consider the impact of spiritual friends, one of the most basic and helpful relationships in the Christian tradition. These are simply friends who commit to journey together as disciples to encourage one another and hold one another accountable for spiritual growth. Have a conversation this week with a friend about developing this kind of partnership.

JOURNAL REFLECTION: Who could you partner with on your spiritual journey (or who are you partnering with already)? How might (or does) that kind of relationship support your growth? What do you have to offer a spiritual friend? What insights did you gain from the conversation you had?

_____

_____

_____

_____

_____

_____

_____

_____

Activity 3:
Beginning
Being Open to Jesus

OPENING TO JESUS

GOAL: Learn to use a Breath Prayer.

Be still before the Lord and wait patiently for him. —Psalm 37:7 (NIV)

ACTION: A struggle many people experience when entering into a time of prayer is that instead of focusing on God, our minds begins to race with all the normal distractions of life (the thing we forgot at the grocery store, the person we need to call, or an insight on a project on which we are working). This is normal, and it's not a sin. One thing that is helpful is to acknowledge these things and even take a moment to write them down so we don't have to keep focusing on them.

A prayer practice that helps us center on our time with God is a Centering Prayer technique called the **Breath Prayer.** It is very simple and usually very effective. This prayer consists of these steps:

• Take a deep breath in and as you do, imagine breathing in the very presence of God (often referred to as the Spirit of God or even wind of the Spirit).
• As you breathe out, consciously release to God all those distractions and concerns. Repeat this process several times until you find yourself able to focus (be centered) on your time with God.

JOURNAL REFLECTION: How did this work for you? What was your experience with being really focused on God?

_____

_____

_____

_____

_____

Activity 4:
Beginning Obedience

 OBEDIENCE

 GOAL: Experience your ordinary life through the lens of "the little way."

> *Therefore, I urge you, brothers and sisters, in view of God's mercy, to offer your bodies as a living sacrifice, holy and pleasing to God—this is your true and proper worship.* —Romans 12:1 (NIV)

 ACTION: St. Therese of Liseaux was a Catholic nun, born in France in the late 1800s. Having a strong passion for serving God and originally dreaming of epic adventures of faith, she came to embrace the holiness of serving in small ways and honoring God in the daily tasks of existence as a way to show her love to others. She called this way of living—of identifying the holiness of every chore and embracing the joy of every relational interaction, no matter how mundane—as "the little way," and so powerful was her witness, that she was eventually canonized as a saint. List some of your daily tasks and routine interactions and how they might be experienced as holy territory.

 JOURNAL REFLECTION: How would thinking about the day-to-day details of life in this manner allow you to experience God's blessings differently? How would this approach make you a more effective conduit of God's love? Be as specific as possible.

_____

_____

_____

_____

_____

_____

_____

_____

_____

Activity 5:
Beginning Service

SERVICE

GOAL: Consider your professional skills and how they can serve God.

Whatever your hand finds to do, do it with all your might, for in the realm of the dead, where you are going, there is neither working nor planning nor knowledge nor wisdom.
—Ecclesiastes 9:10 (NIV)

ACTION: There's a lot of talk in Christian circles about the importance of spiritual gifts. We think they are important as well. However, God's preparation of us for ministry (anything we do to make a Kingdom difference) is bigger than spiritual gifts. God also uses our life experiences. For example, if you do strategic planning as part of your job/career, God can use that skill for helping the church move forward. If you enjoy cooking, God can use that skill to make a difference. The options are endless!

JOURNAL REFLECTION: What life experiences do you have that could benefit the work of the church and make a Kingdom difference? Are you already using these experiences or practical job skills? If so, how? What are examples you see of other people using their professional knowledge to serve the church?

_____

_____

_____

_____

_____

_____

_____

_____

_____

_____

Activity 6:
Beginning Generosity

GENEROSITY

GOAL: Make an honest and forthright assessment of your priorities.

> *And do not set your heart on what you will eat or drink; do not worry about it. For the pagan world runs after all such things, and your Father knows that you need them. But seek his kingdom, and these things will be given to you as well.* —Luke 12:29-31 (NIV)

ACTION: Conversation about generosity is often focused around how much money we give to help others. But generosity is much more. For example, it includes not only how we use our money but also our time and our talents. One way to get a thorough, clear, and honest overview of the generosity level in your life, is to do this: go to your checkbook, your calendar, and your credit card statements, and take a week or a month and see what is most important by the evidence of where you spend money and your time.

JOURNAL REFLECTION: What seems to be the priority as you look at the activities on your calendar? Your checkbook? Your credit card statements? What does this tell you about the level of generosity in your life?

_____

_____

_____

_____

_____

_____

_____

_____

_____

BEGINNING

~ ~ ~ ~ ~

Part 6

Activity 1: Beginning Worship

WORSHIP

GOAL: Experience God's presence as the breath of life.

> *The Spirit of God has made me; the breath of the Almighty gives me life.*
> *—Job 33:4 (NIV)*

ACTION: Consider the words of the popular praise song "The Air I Breathe" (sing it if you are familiar with the song). You are highly encouraged to go online to YouTube and search for a version you can listen to or sing along.

> This is the air I breathe. This is the air I breathe.
> Your holy presence living in me.
>
> This is my daily bread. This is my daily bread.
> Your very Word spoken to me.
>
> And I, I'm desperate for you.
> And I, I'm lost without you.

JOURNAL REFLECTION: What does Matt Redmon, the songwriter, hope to communicate with this song? What would it mean to live life this way, breathing God's holy presence like air?

_____

_____

_____

_____

_____

_____

_____

Activity 2:
Beginning Hospitality

HOSPITALITY

GOAL: Take part in a Prayer Walk in your community.

> *Also, seek the peace and prosperity of the city to which I have carried you into exile. Pray to the LORD for it, because if it prospers, you too will prosper.*
> *—Jeremiah 29:7 (NIV)*

ACTION: We often think about prayer in terms of time in the prayer closet (your quiet space) alone with God. At the opposite end of the spectrum, in terms of the physicality of prayer time, is a technique called a Prayer Walk. In a Prayer Walk, we move with purpose through our neighborhood or town seeking to see the community as God sees it.   When we decide to Prayer Walk as individuals or as communities of faith, we are seeking to connect in a deeper way with the communities in which we live, and we are inviting God to speak to us. We are asking God to show us what we have failed to see. We are asking God to give us new eyes to see what has become invisible to us over time, and new ears to hear what has become white noise to us.

The act of walking gives our bodies something to do. The walking is a sort of calming distraction so that our minds and our souls can focus on listening to God. Schedule a Prayer Walk in your community this week.

JOURNAL REFLECTION: What did God reveal to you? What did you hear? What did you see? What new insights did you gain about neighbors? How did you feel differently about your community when your walk was completed?

_____

_____

_____

_____

_____

Activity 3:
Beginning
Being Open to Jesus

OPENING TO JESUS

GOAL: Use the prayer technique known as the Jesus Prayer.

[Jesus speaking]: "But the tax collector stood at a distance. He would not even look up to heaven, but beat his breast and said, 'God, have mercy on me, a sinner.'"
—Luke 18:13 (NIV)

ACTION: Last week you were invited to try the spiritual practice of the **Breath Prayer**. Many disciples combine this way of centering with what is called the **Jesus Prayer**. It goes like this:

> Lord Jesus Christ, Son of God,
> Have mercy on me, a sinner.

Combined with the Breath Prayer:
- As you repeat the words "Lord Jesus Christ, Son of God," breathe in, visualizing the life-giving breath of God flowing into you.
- As you repeat the words "Have mercy on me, a sinner," exhale, visualizing all of the distractions and concerns of the day flowing away from you.

Try this method of centering prayer this week during your devotional time.

JOURNAL REFLECTION: What was your experience? How did the repetition deepen your sense of the prayer time? Were you able to let your cares and concerns go as you focused on God's mercy?

_____

_____

_____

_____

_____

_____

Activity 4:
Beginning Obedience

OBEDIENCE

GOAL: Use the S.O.A.P. framework to study and reflect on Scripture.

> *Blessed is the one who does not walk in step with the wicked or stand in the way that sinners take or sit in the company of mockers, but whose delight is in the law of the Lord, and who meditates on his law day and night.*
>
> *That person is like a tree planted by streams of water, which yields its fruit in season, and whose leaf does not wither— whatever they do prospers.*
> *Not so the wicked! They are like chaff that the wind blows away.*
>
> *Therefore, the wicked will not stand in the judgment, nor sinners in the assembly of the righteous. For the Lord watches over the way of the righteous, but the way of the wicked leads to destruction. —Psalm 1:1-6 (NIV)*

ACTION: A powerful tool for Bible study/reflection is the S.O.A.P framework. It is an acronym for:

- Scripture: Read the text.
- Observation: What does it communicate to you?
- Application: How does it apply to your life?
- Prayer: Pray for the wisdom to understand and the courage to live as the text indicates.

Try this framework with the Psalm 1 passage above.

JOURNAL REFLECTION: What did you learn? Did using this tool help you dig more deeply into the Scripture passage? How are you called to live?

_____

_____

_____

_____

_____

Activity 5:
Beginning Service

GOAL: Determine whether you are an introvert or extrovert and consider why it matters.

> *But Moses said before the Lord, "Behold, I am unskilled in speech; how then will Pharaoh listen to me?" —Exodus 6:30 (NIV)*

ACTION: There are lots of ways to make a Kingdom difference and lots of ways we can be blessed in the process. The reverse is also true. Sometimes we can be drained by the experience. Much of this is based on where we find ourselves on the introvert-extrovert scale in our personality. Go to www.quietrev.com and type in "Quiet Revolution Personality Test" to find a test to discover where you are on this scale.

We can be most effective in our ministry when we work out of the strengths of our gifts and even the strengths of our personality. This does not limit what we do, only how we do it. For example, someone gifted as a teacher may be very effective in front of a classroom operating as an extrovert. Another person gifted in teaching may be frightened to even think of that experience. However, that person can still use the teaching gift in a way that recognizes personality traits. For example, their focus could be on curriculum development or working one-on-one with someone.

JOURNAL REFLECTION: Where did you place yourself on the introvert—extrovert spectrum? What might this mean for the ways in which you are most comfortable serving? Does this knowledge offer you some relief from guilt about not serving in specific ways?

_____

_____

_____

_____

_____

_____

Activity 6:
Beginning Generosity

GENEROSITY

GOAL: Consider the ways you are already a blessing to others.

The LORD had said to Abram, "Go from your country, your people and your father's household to the land I will show you. I will make you into a great nation, and I will bless you; I will make your name great, and you will be a blessing." —Genesis 12:1-2 (NIV)

ACTION: In Genesis chapter 12, where we read the account of God calling Abram (later Abraham) to become the Father of the people of God, it is made clear that not only would the people be blessed themselves, but that they were being called to be a blessing to others. (Read these verses in your Bible).

JOURNAL REFLECTION: What are some ways you are a 'blessing' to others in your family, your church, your neighborhood? Be specific.

_____

_____

_____

_____

_____

_____

_____

_____

_____

GROWING

~ ~ ~ ~ ~

Part 1

Activity 1:
Growing Worship

WORSHIP

GOAL: Consider the ways you love God with you heart, soul, mind, and strength.

> *One of the teachers of religious law was standing there listening to the debate. He realized that Jesus had answered well, so he asked, "Of all the commandments, which is the most important?" Jesus replied, "The most important commandment is this: 'Listen, O Israel! The Lord our God is the one and only Lord. And you must love the Lord your God with all your heart, all your soul, all your mind, and all your strength.'"*
> —Mark 12:28-30 (NIV)

ACTION: In this passage from Mark, Jesus reminds us that the greatest commandment is to love God with our heart, soul, mind, and strength. In the graphic below consider ways that you live into each of these dimensions:

Heart (affection)	Soul (desire for union with God)
Mind (search for truth/understanding)	Strength (action and serving)

JOURNAL REFLECTION: Which motivation is strongest? Weakest? How does understanding these motivations more fully affect your attitude of worship?

_____

_____

_____

_____

_____

_____

_____

Activity 2:
Growing Hospitality

GOAL: Take an honest look at how well you know your neighbors.

The second is this: 'Love your neighbor as yourself.' There is no commandment greater than these." —Mark 12:31 (NIV)

ACTION: The second commandment that Jesus reminded us about is that of loving our neighbors. Consider the following depiction of your neighborhood. Respond to the questions about your neighbors.

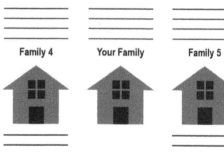

- Can you address all family members by name?
- Do you know what the career(s) are of the parent(s)?
- Have you been in each other's homes? Had a real conversation?
- Have you shared a meal with that family?

How many of the families were you able to respond 'yes' to all questions for? What does this say about your 'love of neighbor'?

JOURNAL REFLECTION: What does this tell you about your love for neighbor? What might be a strong next step in building this love?

_____

_____

_____

_____

_____

_____

_____

_____

Activity 3:
Growing
Being Open to Jesus

OPENING TO JESUS

GOAL: Pray the Lord's Prayer with a line-by-line meditation.

Matthew 6:9-13 (read in your favorite translation)

ACTION: When the disciples asked Jesus to teach them how to pray, he gave them a prayer framework known as the Lord's Prayer, which we have previously utilized in this book. It is often recited in corporate worship and encouraged as a prayer for devotional time. But its most accurate application is to use it as a model or guideline for organizing our petitions to God. Try this expanded framework as a way to organize your prayers this week:

Our Father in heaven *How do you sense the loving presence of the Father (whom Jesus called Abba/Daddy) in your life today? What do you long for?*

Hallowed be your name *How might God's name be lifted up, made holy in your life?*

Your kingdom come *Where, in your life, is there a need for God's reign?*

Your will be done *What guidance are your seeking from God?*

On earth as it is in heaven *Where is the gap between heaven and earth that needs to be filled by the presence of God?*

Give us today our daily bread *What needs do you have that only God can provide?*

And forgive us our debts (trespasses) *What do you need to confess to God, that you might be forgiven?*

As we also have forgiven our debtors (those who trespass against us) *Whom do you need to forgive?*

And lead us not into temptation *What temptations are you facing today?*

But deliver us from evil *Where do you need God's protection?*

For yours is the kingdom and the power and the glory forever *Praise God.*

JOURNAL REFLECTION: What was your experience praying the Lord's prayer in this manner?

_____

_____

_____

_____

_____

Activity 4:
Growing Obedience

OBEDIENCE

GOAL: Consider forgiveness.

> *Be kind and compassionate to one another, forgiving each other, just as in Christ God forgave you.* —Ephesians 4:32 (NIV)

ACTION: This, in essence, is an invitation to 'be who you are.' As disciples, we are a people who have been forgiven. Our response to that is to be the kind of people who are kind and compassionate and forgiving. To forgive is not the same thing as forgetting. It is a choice to instead not hold the offending act or words against someone. It is choosing not to let the trespass destroy the relationship.

JOURNAL REFLECTION: Who has wronged you in some way—through word or deed? Be specific. What would it look like to forgive them? What are the obstacles to practicing forgiveness in this case? What makes it hard?

_____

_____

_____

_____

_____

_____

_____

_____

_____

Activity 5:
Growing Service

SERVICE

GOAL: Serve a neighbor in a simple and straightforward way.

[Jesus speaking:] "The greatest among you will be your servant."
—Matthew 23:11 (NIV)

ACTION: Oftentimes, when we think of service to others, images of mission trips to other countries come to mind, or perhaps we think of community service projects sponsored by the church. Yet, one of the ways we are called to love our neighbors is to serve them simply or directly in some way. It could be providing a meal during a time of crisis, or helping with a lawn project, or taking care of the kids. Look for an opportunity this week to serve someone in your neighborhood. We did an earlier activity based on a simple act of service, but this one encourages you to focus directly on a neighbor (someone who lives next door or nearby).

JOURNAL REFLECTION: What did you do? What was the response of the neighbor you served? How did this make you feel?

_____

_____

_____

_____

_____

_____

_____

_____

Activity 6:
Growing Generosity

GENEROSITY

GOAL: Consider the creation of margin.

When you reap the harvest of your land, do not reap to the very edges of your field or gather the gleanings of your harvest. —Leviticus 19:9 (NIV)

ACTION: In the Hebrew Scriptures (Old Testament), the people of God were called to take care of the needy in their community, as noted in this passage from Leviticus. This was the way of the ancients, practicing financial discipline so that margin could be created and resources made available for God's work. In this agrarian society, the owners of land were encouraged not to harvest all the way to the edges but to leave some for the poor in order that they might be cared for. For modern day disciples, we are encouraged to do this with our financial resources—spending less than what God has made available to us—in order to respond to observed needs.

JOURNAL REFLECTION: How might you create some margin around the edges of your spending? What amount could you set aside in order to respond to needs around you? How would this change your attitudes about giving when opportunities to give arise?

_____

_____

_____

_____

_____

_____

_____

_____

GROWING

~ ~ ~ ~ ~

Part 2

Activity 1:
Growing Worship

 WORSHIP

 GOAL: Reflect on personal examples of reasons you love the Lord.

> *I love the Lord, for he heard my voice;*
>   *he heard my cry for mercy.*
> *Because he turned his ear to me,*
>   *I will call on him as long as I live. —Psalm 116:1-2 (NIV)*

 ACTION: The psalmist shares these words at the very beginning of Psalm 116: "I love the Lord, for. . . ." (read that as *because . . . I love the Lord because*). Complete this phrase as it applies to your life. What are the ways God has supported you?

 JOURNAL REFLECTION: Write down your own version of Psalm 116, listing the ways God has offered support and sustenance and heard your voice and cries for mercy. Try to write from five to 10 verses.

_____

_____

_____

_____

_____

_____

_____

_____

_____

Activity 2:
Growing Hospitality

 HOSPITALITY

 GOAL: Share how God has been working in your life.

> *But in your hearts revere Christ as Lord. Always be prepared to give an answer to everyone who asks you to give the reason for the hope that you have.* — 1 Peter 3:15a (NIV)

 **ACTION:** : These words from the apostle, Peter, are a reminder that we should always be prepared to share the Good News of what God has done for us, personally. Have a conversation with a friend this week about how you have seen God at work in your life. Where has God helped you through difficult times? Provided guidance? Blessed you in a particular way?

 JOURNAL REFLECTION: What was it like to share God's work in your own life? Was it more difficult than talking about a new restaurant you recently found or a new movie you really like? Why or why not? What was your friend's reaction to what you shared?

_____

_____

_____

_____

_____

_____

_____

_____

_____

Activity 3:
Growing
Being Open to Jesus

OPENING TO JESUS

GOAL: Read the Scriptures like a reporter.

The unfolding of your words gives light; it gives understanding to the simple.
—Psalm 119:130 (NIV)

ACTION: Journalists are often taught that when they report on anything, they need to answer six basic questions about every story. These same basic questions help us to understand more deeply what is going on in the stories told in the Bible. Pick a New Testament story you know well or one you do not know at all and try working your way through these questions:

Who? Can you identify who is in this story? How are they described? What are the characters' relationships to each other?

When? When does this story take place? How much time passes in the story? How do these events relate to other events chronologically?

Where? Where does the story take place? How is the place described?

What? What happens in the story? What issues or topics are raised by the passage?

Why? Why does what happens happen? What motivates the people in the story to do what they do? Why does the author tell the story?

How? How do these events unfold? How do they relate to each other? How do they relate to other events in the Bible?

And finally...

So What? What does this story tell you? How does this story help you understand something about your own life, the people you know, God, or Jesus?

JOURNAL REFLECTION: What story did you choose? What did you discover? Was this method of thinking about the story in more detail helpful for you?

_____

_____

_____

_____

_____

Activity 4:
Growing Obedience

 **OBEDIENCE**

 GOAL: Move beyond rules to a place of obedience through God's presence and power.

> *Therefore, my dear friends, as you have always obeyed—not only in my presence, but now much more in my absence—continue to work out your salvation with fear and trembling, for it is God who works in you to will and to act in order to fulfill his good purpose. —Philippians 2:12-13 (NIV)*

 **ACTION:** Paul is calling the believers to be steadfast in their obedience to the teachings through which they discover salvation (a fullness of life in Christ). One might be tempted to think that this is just another way of encouraging rule following. But it is much more than that. How does the text describe the way in which we are able to fully live into the teachings of God's Word? What does it mean to "work out your salvation"?

 **JOURNAL REFLECTION:** Describe an example where you have not had the power within to be obedient, but were supported by the very presence of God. Be specific.

_____

_____

_____

_____

_____

_____

_____

_____

_____

_____

Activity 5:
Growing Service

 SERVICE

 GOAL: Research opportunities for service in your community (and beyond your church).

> [Jesus speaking:] *"In the same way, let your light shine before others, that they may see your good deeds and glorify your Father in heaven".* —Matthew 5:16 (NIV)

 ACTION: Use online resources, local print publications, and conversations with friends and coworkers to explore opportunities to serve in your community beyond the service options and ministries directly sponsored by your church. Write down your findings. There are many parachurch organizations (not sponsored by a specific congregation or denomination) like Habitat for Humanity, and there are many fine organizations that have nothing to do with churches, synagogues, or mosques at all. Schools are always looking for tutors; homeless shelters are looking for help; and hospitals need assistance. See how many different options you can come up with in your city or town.

 JOURNAL REFLECTION: What did you learn in your search? How are some of these opportunities to serve different than the ones that your local congregation routinely offers? What do you see that particularly intrigues you? What challenges or opportunities do you expect you might encounter if you serve in a non-religious-institution-sponsored organization? (If you already serve in such a capacity, use that service to inform your responses.)

_____

_____

_____

_____

_____

_____

Activity 6:
Growing Generosity

GENEROSITY

GOAL: Reflect on God's sovereignty and ownership of all.

> *The earth is the Lord's and everything in it;*
> *The world and all who live in it. —Psalm 24:1 (NIV)*

ACTION: We proceed through our lives, working, saving, and acquiring, under the premise that we have earned all that we have gained through our sweat and intellectual prowess, and we are entitled to use it as we deem best. The Bible, however, speaks the truth that all things come from God. God owns it all, and we are in fact merely stewards charged to use our blessings for the good of God's Kingdom.

Do this: take a sheet of labels (or make your own from masking tape), writing "GOD" on 20 of them, then walk around your home placing these labels on your 20 most prized possessions. Now, use these possessions over the next few days, reminding yourself that they are not really yours, but simply on loan from God.

JOURNAL REFLECTION: How does considering your possessions in this way make you rethink your relationship to them? Does it make you think differently about how you use them (how could you use them in more productive, healthy, God-honoring ways)? Does it make you think about how you might have perhaps invested in more Kingdom appropriate decisions?

_____

_____

_____

_____

_____

_____

_____

GROWING

✦ ✦ ✦ ✦ ✦

Part 3

Activity 1:
Growing Worship

 | **WORSHI**

GOAL: Use a candle as a tool for focusing fully on Christ's presence.

> *"Be still, and know that I am God;*
>   *I will be exalted among the nations,*
>   *I will be exalted in the earth." —Psalm 46:10 (NIV)*

ACTION: In your quiet time (daily devotional time) place a candle on a table near where you are seated. Light the candle as a symbol of the presence of Christ. You might even invite/welcome that presence (although Christ is always present) specifically into your space, saying: "Jesus Christ, Light of the World, come."

Take a few minutes to watch the candle. Notice how it flickers with the currents of air in the space. Feel the warmth which emanates from the flame. Hold the candle up and notice how its light casts away the darkness.

Be present to Christ and what Christ wants for you in that moment.

JOURNAL REFLECTION: What insights were revealed to you in this spiritual exercise? How would you describe your experience of the presence of Christ? Does having something real like the flickering candle to focus on enhance your ability to concentrate and pray?

_____

_____

_____

_____

_____

_____

_____

Activity 2:
Growing Hospitality

HOSPITALITY

 GOAL: Imagine practical ways that you can create an atmosphere of invitation and welcome for your neighbors, ways your home can project welcome and community friendliness.

> *Accept one another, then, just as Christ accepted you, in order to bring praise to God.*
> *—Romans 15:7 (NIV)*

 ACTION: Go online to www.kristinschell.com and read the story of how one person, feeling called to connect with her neighbors, started making those connections right away by putting a turquoise picnic table in her front yard and sitting where she could greet people as they walked by. This simple act started a movement around the world of neighbors connecting with neighbors and lives being touched and transformed by the new relationships that resulted.

Jesus calls us to love our neighbor in simple and practical ways.

 JOURNAL REFLECTION: The turquoise table may not be the answer for your neighborhood. But what could you do to begin building relationships and communities of caring right where you live? What signals and signs could you create in your own yard that outwardly communicate your desire to welcome connections? Be as specific as possible.

_____

_____

_____

_____

_____

_____

_____

_____

Activity 3:
Growing
Being Open to Jesus

OPENING TO JESUS

GOAL: Personalize a Scriptural encouragement.

> *...being confident of this, that he who began a good work in you will carry it on to completion until the day of Christ Jesus.* —Philippians 1:6 (NIV)

ACTION: : In your prayer time today pray this verse of Scripture, substituting your own name for the YOU in the text. For example: **I am confident that, Jesus who began a good work in (your name) will carry it on to completion until the day of Jesus Christ.**

Now pray this same verse for a friend.

JOURNAL REFLECTION: How did it feel to express this confidence in the work of Jesus in your life? To pray this way for a friend? How would it change your perceptions if you thought of yourself (and your friend) more regularly in this way?

_____

_____

_____

_____

_____

_____

_____

_____

Activity 4:
Growing Obedience

GOAL: Consider the fruit of the Spirit evidenced by your own life.

But the fruit of the Spirit is love, joy, peace, patience, kindness, goodness, faithfulness, gentleness, self-control. . . . —Colossians 5:22-23 (NIV)

ACTION: : The fruit of the Spirit refers to the ways that the working of the Holy Spirit is evidenced in our lives. Note that it says 'fruit' and not 'fruits'. That means that all of these together in aggregate are the evidence of the Spirit at work in our lives, rather than some you-pick-'em arrangement by which we choose the specific fruit we endorse (or find easiest) and set the others aside.

JOURNAL REFLECTION: Which of these 'fruit' are most evident in your life? How is this demonstrated? Which 'fruit' do you struggle with the most?

_____

_____

_____

_____

_____

_____

_____

_____

_____

Activity 5:
Growing Service

SERVICE

GOAL: Explore the characteristics that identify servant leaders.

Now in these days when the disciples were increasing in number, the Hellenists murmured against the Hebrews because their widows were neglected in the daily distribution. And the twelve summoned the body of the disciples and said, "It is not right that we should give up preaching the Word of God to serve tables. Therefore, brethren, pick out from among you seven men of good repute, full of the Spirit and of wisdom, whom we may appoint to this duty. But we will devote ourselves to prayer and to the ministry of the word." And what they said pleased the whole multitude, and they chose Stephen, a man full of faith and of the Holy Spirit, and Philip, and Prochorus, and Nicanor, and Timon, and Parmenas, and Nicolaus, a proselyte of Antioch. These they set before the apostles, and they prayed and laid their hands upon them. And the word of God increased; and the number of the disciples multiplied greatly in Jerusalem, and a great many of the priests were obedient to the faith. —Acts 6:1-7 (NIV)

ACTION: This text introduces to the Christian community the idea of servant leadership. Take a moment to read through the text again more closely. What was the issue being addressed? How was it resolved? Embedded in the text are the characteristics that were identified by the Apostles for those being identified as servant leaders for the community.

JOURNAL REFLECTION: Circle the characteristics of servant leaders that you identified. How well do these describe you? Give examples of why or why not for each characteristic.

_____

_____

_____

_____

Activity 6:
Growing Generosity

GENEROSITY

GOAL: Consider the quality of what you offer God.

> [Jesus speaking:] *"But seek first his kingdom and his righteousness, and all these things will be given to you as well."* —Matthew 6:33 (NIV)

ACTION: This promise from Jesus comes at the end of a chapter in which he has exhorted his listeners to give to the needy, to pray with sincerity, and to stop fixating on their material needs. First things first, and our first priority as disciples is to honor the God we serve with the firstfruits of our lives: the best of who we are and what we have to offer. That means, we set aside time for God as our top priority; we present our offerings to God and live on the rest; we take care of Godly things first, and all else will fall into place.

We earlier engaged in an activity to help us take a clear look at our priorities. Now let's look at the quality of what we're offering of ourselves and our households. Are we offering the best or the leftovers? Do an analysis of what you've offered up to God in the past month. Write down examples of how you offered God time, talent, gifts, service, and witness. Were these your very best efforts or what you had energy left to do so you could say you checked the box?

JOURNAL REFLECTION: By conducting a thoughtful analysis (backed by evidence), did you gain any insights about the perception of what you're offering to God versus the reality of what you're offering to God? How could you take steps, change habits, or develop new disciplines to ensure that you're offering up the best of who and what you are?

_____

_____

_____

_____

_____

GROWING

~ ~ ~ ~ ~

Part 4

Activity 1: Growing Worship

WORSHIP

GOAL: Imagine the work of the divine potter in your life.

This is the word that came to Jeremiah from the Lord: "Go down to the potter's house, and there I will give you my message." So I went down to the potter's house, and I saw him working at the wheel. But the pot he was shaping from the clay was marred in his hands; so the potter formed it into another pot, shaping it as seemed best to him. Then the word of the Lord came to me. He said, "Can I not do with you, Israel, as this potter does?" declares the Lord. "Like clay in the hand of the potter, so are you in my hand, Israel." —Jeremiah 18:1-6 (NIV)

ACTION: Take a piece of clay or Play-Doh and form it to make an object of your choice. As you read this text a second time, slowly and carefully, flatten the object you created and form a second object. Imagine the Lord taking your life and forming and reforming it.

JOURNAL REFLECTION: Where can you see the divine potter at work as you look back on your journey?

_____

_____

_____

_____

_____

_____

_____

Activity 2:
Growing Hospitality

 HOSPITALITY

 GOAL: Love your neighbor as you love yourself.

> On one occasion an expert in the law stood up to test Jesus. "Teacher," he asked, "what must I do to inherit eternal life?"
>
> "What is written in the Law?" he replied. "How do you read it?"
>
> He answered, "'Love the Lord your God with all your heart and with all your soul and with all your strength and with all your mind'; and, 'Love your neighbor as yourself.'"
>
> You have answered correctly," Jesus replied. "Do this and you will live."
>
> —*Luke 10:25-28 (NIV)*

 ACTION: Earlier we saw this exchange as recorded in Mark, now we see the Luke version. Explore a new perspective on loving your neighbor as you love yourself by taking that guidance literally. Think of a way you might normally treat or reward yourself and instead do that thing for your neighbor (spend the funds you might have spent on yourself on a neighbor instead). Maybe you buy them a pie or treat them to movie tickets or pay the kid down the street to mow their lawn or have their car detailed.

 JOURNAL REFLECTION: What neighbor did you serve? What action of "loving your neighbor" did you choose? How did it make you feel? What response did you receive from the neighbor? What was it like to do something you might have done for yourself for someone else?

_____

_____

_____

_____

_____

_____

_____

Activity 3:
Growing
Being Open to Jesus

OPENING TO JESUS

GOAL: Pray a biblically inspired prayer.

> *Jabez cried out to the God of Israel, "Oh, that you would bless me and enlarge my territory! Let your hand be with me, and keep me from harm so that I will be free from pain." And God granted his request.* —1 Chronicles 4:10 (NIV)

ACTION: The Bible is full of prayers by the people of God. Some of them can be examples of how to pray, and others can be prayed by us even today. The prayer of Jabez is an example of praying the prayers of the Bible.

JOURNAL REFLECTION: What blessing are you seeking from God? How might God enlarge your territory (circle of influence)? What do you need protection from?

_____

_____

_____

_____

_____

_____

_____

_____

Activity 4:
Growing Obedience

GOAL: Consider how disciples are like salt.

> [Jesus speaking:] "You are the salt of the earth. But if the salt loses its saltiness, how can it be made salty again? It is no longer good for anything, except to be thrown out and trampled underfoot." —Matthew 5:13 (NIV)

ACTION: Jesus calls the disciples the "salt" of the earth. In ancient times salt was used to preserve foods as well as to enhance the flavor of foods. Calling disciples salt is a metaphor for the disciples preserving a Kingdom way of life and enhancing the experience of life. Pour a little salt in your hand and hold it there while you read this Scripture again slowly. Then release the salt onto the table and consider each grain as an opportunity for how you can be a "salty servant."

JOURNAL REFLECTION: As you consider your life, what about you preserves (witnesses to) a Kingdom way of life? To bringing flavor to life? How could that witness be strengthened?

_____

_____

_____

_____

_____

_____

_____

_____

_____

Activity 5:
Growing Service

SERVICE

GOAL: In the spirit of Christ, serve someone less fortunate.

> [Jesus speaking:] "When the Son of Man comes in his glory, and all the angels with him, he will sit on his glorious throne. All the nations will be gathered before him, and he will separate the people one from another as a shepherd separates the sheep from the goats. He will put the sheep on his right and the goats on his left.
>
> "Then the King will say to those on his right, 'Come, you who are blessed by my Father; take your inheritance, the kingdom prepared for you since the creation of the world. For I was hungry and you gave me something to eat, I was thirsty and you gave me something to drink, I was a stranger and you invited me in, I needed clothes and you clothed me, I was sick and you looked after me, I was in prison and you came to visit me.'
>
> "Then the righteous will answer him, 'Lord, when did we see you hungry and feed you, or thirsty and give you something to drink? When did we see you a stranger and invite you in, or needing clothes and clothe you? When did we see you sick or in prison and go to visit you?' The King will reply, 'Truly I tell you, whatever you did for one of the least of these brothers and sisters of mine, you did for me.'"
> —Matthew 25:31-40 (NIV)

ACTION: Jesus reminds us that a central calling in the life of a disciple is to serve those less fortunate. The early Methodists took this to heart as they built into their covenant relationship the specific task of helping someone in need each week. Find someone who fits the description of one of the needs mentioned above and reach out to them in a tangible way.

JOURNAL REFLECTION: How did you help someone less fortunate than you? What was the impact for them and for you? What are the challenges inherent in helping another person?

_____
_____
_____
_____

Activity 6:
Growing Generosity

GENEROSITY

GOAL: Remember the Sabbath.

Remember the Sabbath day by keeping it holy. Six days you shall labor and do all your work, but the seventh day is a sabbath to the LORD your God. On it you shall not do any work, neither you, nor your son or daughter, nor your male or female servant, nor your animals, nor any foreigner residing in your towns. For in six days the LORD made the heavens and the earth, the sea, and all that is in them, but he rested on the seventh day. Therefore the LORD blessed the Sabbath day and made it holy. —Exodus 20:8-11 (NIV)

ACTION: In the Ten Commandments, found in Exodus chapter 20, God includes the keeping of the Sabbath. This is a day where no work was to be done (The Israelites were very OCD about how this got lived out). It was a day focused on God and being in community. It was a time to rest from the demands of life and be refreshed.

God set this up for you. In the busyness of our world, even the busyness of the Church, the Sabbath sometimes gets lost. Meditate on what Sabbath means to you. Are you intentional about practicing it? Can you think of an example of someone who is?

JOURNAL REFLECTION: What are some specific ways you could recapture the life-giving practice, this holy practice in your life? What expectations and habits might keep you from living out this restorative practice?

_____

_____

_____

_____

_____

_____

GROWING

~ ~ ~ ~ ~

Part 5

Activity 1:
Growing Worship

 WORSHIP

GOAL: Use Rembrant's "Prodigal Son" painting as a way to explore God's fathomless love.

> *[Jesus speaking:] "But the father said to his servants, 'Quick! Bring the best robe and put it on him. Put a ring on his finger and sandals on his feet. Bring the fattened calf and kill it. Let's have a feast and celebrate. For this son of mine was dead and is alive again; he was lost and is found.' So they began to celebrate." —Luke 15:22-24 (NIV)*

ACTION: Go to www.rembrantpainting.net and select the "Prodigal Son" painting. Click to enlarge the picture and take a few minutes to study it very carefully. What strikes you? What does Rembrant wish to convey?

Read the entire story of the Prodigal Son found in Luke 15:11-32, keeping the visual of the painting in mind. This story is most often referred to as the Prodigal Son or the Lost Son. In a very strong sense, it is really the story of a prodigal God (*prodigal* meaning generous to the point of extravagance or wastefulness). In contrast to the expected response to a wayward son, the father welcomes him home, restores to him all the privileges of being family, and throws a great celebration.

JOURNAL REFLECTION: Jesus describes a God who welcomes us home no matter what we have done, where we have been, and who we have become. Take a moment to celebrate that amazing gift in your life. What does this mean for you?

_____

_____

_____

_____

_____

_____

_____

Activity 2:
Growing Hospitality

 HOSPITALITY

 GOAL: Give an answer for the hope you have (and the place in which you embrace it).

> *Always be prepared to give an answer to everyone who asks you to give the reason for the hope you have.* —1 Peter 3:15 (NIV)

 ACTION: In this verse Peter reminds us that we should always be ready to share the reason for our faith. To help you think this through and be prepared, consider the following questions:

• Why Jesus?
• Why church?
• Why your particular church?

 JOURNAL REFLECTION: For your own faith, for your own denomination, for your own particular house of worship, write down answers for those questions posed above. Why Jesus? Why church? Why your particular church?

_____

_____

_____

_____

_____

_____

_____

_____

_____

Activity 3:
Growing
Being Open to Jesus

OPENING TO JESUS

GOAL: Draw an arboreal illustration to contrast the life that is and the life that might be.

> *They will be like a tree planted by the water that sends out its roots by the stream. It does not fear when heat comes; its leaves are always green. It has no worries in a year of drought and never fails to bear fruit. —Jeremiah 17:8 (NIV)*

ACTION: Reflect carefully on the verse from Jeremiah above, where we are promised that those who study God's law and live by God's Word will be "like trees planted along a riverbank with roots that reach deep."

JOURNAL REFLECTION: In the space below, draw two trees (one on each side of the blank lines). One reflects life as you are currently experiencing it, and the second reflects life as it could be. What would it take for your life to move from its current reality to what it could be? Make notes between the trees from your reflection. Where do you need God to be at work to make this happen?

_____

_____

_____

_____

_____

_____

Activity 4:
Growing Obedience

 **OBEDIENCE**

 GOAL: Form a spiritual friendship.

> *Walk with the wise and become wise, for a companion of fools suffers harm.*
> *—Proverbs 13:20 (NIV)*

 ACTION: The role of spiritual friendships is a time-honored tradition in growing as disciples. It is simply two friends committing to each other to journey together as they seek to grow toward maturity as disciples of Jesus Christ. There is no 'expert' in a spiritual friendship. The spiritual friends agree to meet regularly and share what they are experiencing and learning. They may decide to study Scripture together or share a contemporary resource to help guide them along the path. They encourage and support one another.

 JOURNAL REFLECTION: Who could you partner with to engage in a spiritual friendship? What step could you take this week to make that happen? What might be some things you'd like to explore with a spiritual friend (resources, retreats, topics, ways to serve, etc.)? If you are already part of such a partnership, reflect on its impact on your life.

_____

_____

_____

_____

_____

_____

_____

Activity 5:
Growing Service

GOAL: Serve by praying for your community and the world.

Yet give attention to your servant's prayer and his plea for mercy, Lord my God. Hear the cry and the prayer that your servant is praying in your presence this day.
—1 Kings 8:28 (NIV)

ACTION: We often think of service in terms of activity. While this is generally true, it must also be noted that throughout Christian history (continuing even today) there are communities that are devoted to the specific service of praying for the needs of people (monastic communities/convents). Consider the following guide to praying for our world:

Together, let us pray for
the people of this congregation . . .
those who suffer and those in trouble . . .
the concerns of this local community . . .
the world, its people, and its leaders . . .
the church universal—its leaders, its members, and its mission . . .
the communion of saints.
    —The United Methodist Hymnal

JOURNAL REFLECTION: Using this framework, serve your world this week by praying for the needs of the world. What did God reveal or bring to mind for you? Try responding line by line.

_____

_____

_____

_____

Activity 6: Growing Generosity

GENEROSITY

GOAL: Name ways in which you are blessed (rather than deprived).

> *You will be enriched in every way so that you can be generous on every occasion, and through us your generosity will result in thanksgiving to God.*
> *—2 Corinthians 9:11 (NIV)*

ACTION: Our generosity, as disciples of Jesus Christ, is a response to how God has blessed us. It is a way of saying thanks to God as we read above in Paul's words to the Corinthians. In a world where we are bombarded with a mindset of scarcity (in which we are constantly prodded that we don't have enough), we are called to live out of a mindset of abundance. We have all been blessed beyond measure.

JOURNAL REFLECTION: List at least five things that you have to be thankful for. Focus on the world's perspective that you don't have enough—that you should desire more. Contrast it with the counter-argument that you are actually blessed. Give God thanks!

_____

_____

_____

_____

_____

_____

_____

GROWING

Part 6

Activity 1:
Growing Worship

WORSHIP

GOAL: Explore worship beyond the worship service.

> *Through Jesus, therefore, let us continually offer up a sacrifice of praise to God, that is, the fruit of our lips that give thanks to His name. And do not neglect doing good and sharing, for with such sacrifices God is pleased. —Hebrews 13:15-16 (NIV)*

ACTION: The most common image for worship is the gathering of believers in a corporate setting for a time of praise, prayer, and proclamation (teaching). This is a healthy practice for disciples. There is great value in gathering to celebrate what God is doing in our midst. However, worship is bigger than gathering for a weekend event. Worship is a lifestyle where everything we do is an opportunity to bring honor and glory to God.

Intentionally engage in some form of sharing this week (conversation with someone, meeting a need), and think of approaching this interaction as an act of worship. Make it a conversation that offers hope or gives someone a chance to share their struggles with you.

JOURNAL REFLECTION: Briefly recount the content of this conversation. How did this bring honor and glory to God?

_____

_____

_____

_____

_____

_____

_____

_____

Activity 2:
Growing Hospitality

HOSPITALITY

GOAL: Take the Real Discipleship Survey—see how your journey progresses.

To this you were called, because Christ suffered for you, leaving you an example, that you should follow in his steps. —1 Peter 2:21 (NIV)

ACTION: Take the Real Discipleship Survey found at www.emc3coaching.com/store. Read through the report provided. Talk with your spiritual partner, group leader, or coach about possible next steps in your journey as a disciple.

JOURNAL REFLECTION: What most surprised you about your results from the Real Discipleship Survey? What was most encouraging to you? Why do you think you have progressed farther in some areas than others?

Activity 3:
Growing
Being Open to Jesus

OPENING TO JESUS

GOAL: Find inspiration for your spiritual walk in Christian movies, drama, poetry, or fiction.

> *Above all else, guard your heart, for everything you do flows from it.*
> *—Proverbs 4:23 (NIV)*

ACTION: There are many Christian writers, artists, and filmmakers who bring the struggles of discipleship to life in dramatic ways. These creative works can explore questions of faith through powerfully relevant stories and can inspire us, convict us, or lead us to see things we haven't seen before. Make a list of some of your favorite movies, novels, plays or poetry that have worked in this way for you. Then, experience a new creative work that deals with a question of faith (publications and web sites such as ChristianityToday.com, Crosswalk.com, as well as a standard internet search, offer a lots of suggestions). Pick something out to watch or read (make it a family project if applicable!)

JOURNAL REFLECTION: What did you choose? In what ways did your choice move you to think more deeply about your faith walk? What works have been favorites in your development as a disciple? What would you recommend to others? How do mainstream entertainment choices influence our discipleship (for good or ill)?

_____

_____

_____

_____

_____

_____

_____

_____

Activity 4:
Growing Obedience

 OBEDIENCE

GOAL: Visit a small group. Consider the ways in which they enhance accountable discipleship.

> *And let us consider how we may spur one another on toward love and good deeds, not giving up meeting together, as some are in the habit of doing, but encouraging one another—and all the more as you see the Day approaching.*
> —Hebrews 10:24-25 (NIV)

ACTION: One of the most helpful activities in the life of a growing disciple is participation in a small discipleship group. The participants develop stronger relationships, provide support and encouragement, challenge one another, and hold each other accountable. This is a practice in line with a strong Christian tradition from ancient times. Visit a small group this week and consider the benefits for your growth as a disciple. (If you are already part of a small group, consider visiting another small group and note the similarities and differences between that group and yours.)

JOURNAL REFLECTION: What are the ways in which small group participation has made you a stronger disciple? If you were visiting a new small group, what were your observations about the interactions of the group members and the accountability reflected there?

_____

_____

_____

_____

_____

_____

_____

_____

_____

Activity 5:
Growing Service

SERVICE

GOAL: Explore the idea of presence.

> *Therefore if you have any encouragement from being united with Christ, if any comfort from his love, if any common sharing in the Spirit, if any tenderness and compassion, then make my joy complete by being like-minded, having the same love, being one in spirit and of one mind. Do nothing out of selfish ambition or vain conceit. Rather, in humility value others above yourselves, not looking to your own interests but each of you to the interests of the others. —Philippians 2:1-4 (NIV)*

ACTION: Henri Nouwen, a priest and renowned author, wrote this passage:

> It is a privilege to practice this simple ministry of presence . . . still it is not as simple as it seems. . . . I wonder . . . if the first things shouldn't be to know people by name, to eat and drink with them, to listen to their stories and tell your own. . . and let them know that you do not simply like them—but truly love them.

What opportunity is there for you to connect with people with whom you wouldn't normally engage (e.g. food pantry, soup kitchen, shelter for the homeless, person asking for change at an intersection, etc.)? Take an opportunity this week to actually have a conversation with someone being served in this way.

JOURNAL REFLECTION: With whom did you have a conversation? (How difficult was it to find someone who was being served in this way with whom you could have this conversation?) What insights did you gain? What is the value of such presence?

_____

_____

_____

_____

Activity 6:
Growing Generosity

GENEROSITY

GOAL: Give something up and use the resources instead to support a ministry.

> *By faith Moses, when he had grown up, refused to be known as the son of Pharaoh's daughter. He chose to be mistreated along with the people of God rather than to enjoy the fleeting pleasures of sin. He regarded disgrace for the sake of Christ as of greater value than the treasures of Egypt, because he was looking ahead to his reward. By faith he left Egypt, not fearing the king's anger; he persevered because he saw him who is invisible. —Hebrews 11:24-27 (NIV)*

ACTION: Most people want to do good and like the idea of giving to support good causes, but they don't see how they can make it happen. One of the keys to a lifestyle of giving is redirecting our discretionary income. It could be as simple as fixing coffee at home rather than stopping by the expensive coffee shop or taking a lunch rather than going out for lunch. Pick something specific in your financial spending habits that you could eliminate for a week. Put those unspent resources aside to support a specific need in your community.

JOURNAL REFLECTION: What did you choose? How faithful were you to this? How much money did you save? What need did you support? How did you feel at the end of this experiment?

_____

_____

_____

_____

_____

_____

_____

MATURING

~ ~ ~ ~ ~

Part 1

Activity 1:
Maturing Worship

WORSHIP

GOAL: Schedule a personal Advance day.

> As the deer pants for streams of water,
>   so my soul pants for you, my God.
> My soul thirsts for God, for the living God.
> When can I go and meet with God? —Psalm 42:1-2 (NIV)

ACTION: Most active church participants are familiar with the term "Retreat." It is usually described as a time to get away and spend some time with God and maybe even do some learning activities. Flipping the script, another way to think about personal renewal is the idea of an "Advance" (a concept popularized by Leonard Sweet). While it includes some time to get away and be alone with God, the Advance is a focused opportunity to pay attention to what God wants for you as you move forward. It is usually just a day spent somewhere away from your normal responsibilities. The Advance includes some time for personal worship, prayer and study, as well as some reflection on your calendar and activities that are coming up in the month ahead. It provides space for God to speak into our lives and direct our path.

Those involved in ministry (professional and laypeople) often get so caught up in the activities that we miss the God-inspired purpose. Many find the Advance to be a way to bring things back into focus.

Look at your calendar for the month and schedule a day apart for your own Advance. Make sure to clear the space from other responsibilities.

JOURNAL REFLECTION: What feelings bubble to the surface when you consider scheduling an Advance? What would make it difficult? What value do you see in making it happen? Where and how will you spend it?

_____

_____

_____

_____

_____

Activity 2:
Maturing Hospitality

 GOAL: Use a symbol timeline to share your story.

> He said to them, "Go into all the world and preach the gospel to all creation. Whoever believes and is baptized will be saved, but whoever does not believe will be condemned."
> —Mark 16:15-16 (NIV)

 ACTION: One of the most effective ways to live into our calling to make disciples, especially when we consider reaching out to those beyond the church walls, is to simply tell our story. To share how God has been at work in our lives.

The symbol timeline is a tool to help you share your story. In each of the circles below, draw an image that reflects a phase in your life journey. This is not an art contest—stick figures work just fine. Note with an arrow a turning point(s) in your journey.

Share your story with a friend. Invite them to share theirs.

 JOURNAL REFLECTION: What was it like sharing your story with a friend? What did you learn about your friend? What was your friend surprised to learn about you?

_____

_____

_____

_____

_____

Activity 3:
Maturing
Being Open to Jesus

OPENING TO JESUS

GOAL: Imagine yourself in a biblical scene.

He got up, took his mat and walked out in full view of them all. This amazed everyone and they praised God, saying, "We have never seen anything like this!"
—Mark 2:12 (NIV)

ACTION: Read the entire passage, Mark 2:1-12, the healing of the paralytic. After you have read and become familiar with the story, enter into a time of quiet reflection. In your mind's eye, picture the scene of this story. Feel the temperature of the day. Visualize the crowds gathered at the house where there is standing room only and people crowding in from outside, hoping just to get a glimpse of Jesus. Picture the men carrying the paralytic and then making a hole in the roof to lower him down into the presence of Jesus.

JOURNAL REFLECTION: What is the response of Jesus? What is the response of the crowd? What does Jesus say to the man? What is Jesus saying to you through this story?

_____

_____

_____

_____

_____

_____

_____

_____

_____

_____

_____

_____

Activity 4:
Maturing Obedience

GOAL: See your neighborhood the way that God sees it.

> [Jesus speaking:] *"For God so loved the world that he gave his one and only Son, that whoever believes in him shall not perish but have eternal life."* —John 3:16 (NIV)

ACTION: This is one of the most familiar and most often memorized passages of Scripture. Consider it in the context of your life by doing these things: walk down your street and back, repeating this Scripture and paying close attention to your surroundings; go shopping at your local grocery store repeating this Scripture and paying close attention to your surroundings; take public transportation, repeating this Scripture and paying close attention to your surroundings.

JOURNAL REFLECTION: Who are these people that God loves so much? What would it mean for you to love these people as God loves them?

Activity 5:
Maturing Service

 SERVICE

GOAL: Volunteer with a neighborhood service group.

Dear children, let us not love with words or speech but with actions and in truth.
—1 John 3:18 (NIV)

ACTION: We often think about service in terms of what the church does to serve people in the community and even the world. However, there are lots of organizations that seek to serve the needs of people right in your community. They may not have the label of church, but they certainly express the love of Jesus through their actions.

Make a connection with a service organization within your community (through your earlier research or through a friend who is already volunteering with an organization). Select one that seems to connect with your passions and gifts. Volunteer to serve in some way. If you are already volunteering, consider serving with a different organization for new experience.

JOURNAL REFLECTION: What volunteer opportunity did you choose? Why? What was the experience like for you? Was it different in any way from working with an explicitly church-sponsored ministry?

_____

_____

_____

_____

_____

_____

_____

Activity 6:
Maturing Generosity

GENEROSITY

GOAL: Consider what it means to use less than is available to you.

> *Those who trust in their riches will fall,*
>   *but the righteous will thrive like a green leaf.*
> *—Proverbs 11:28 (NIV)*

ACTION: It has long been a spiritual practice for the people of God (Hebrew Scriptures and the New Testament) to set aside a portion of what God has provided to help care for those in less fortunate circumstances.

Such giving is not a matter of luck. It is a matter of thoughtful planning and intentionally living, not just within our means, but below our means, so that there is extra for God's work and meeting the needs of others. (This is the previously explored concept of living with margin.)

Do the following experiment: Write down your payments and expenses in areas such as house payment, transportation, food, entertainmenet, etc. For each category, visualize the impact on your life if you reduced that expense by 10%. Then imagine the impact on ministry you could support for those specific categories for someone in need (be as specific as you can—use charitable giving web sites to help).

JOURNAL REFLECTION: What insights did you gain from this exercise? What changes might you make in the future that could put you in a stronger position to support the care of others and the work of God's people? What impact would it have if all God's people lived with margin in this way?

_____

_____

_____

_____

MATURING

~ ~ ~ ~ ~

Part 2

Activity 1: Maturing Worship

 WORSHIP

 GOAL: Experience a different kind of worship.

All the nations you have made will come and worship before you, Lord; they will bring glory to your name. For you are great and do marvelous deeds; you alone are God.
—Psalm 86:9-10 (NIV)

 ACTION: Most people attend the worship experience that is most comfortable. There is nothing wrong with this, of course. But it can limit our experience of God's work in the midst of God's people. Phil, for instance, has been blessed by the joys of worshiping with a Haitian congregation (a three-hour experience where worship didn't begin until everyone arrived). He has worshiped with a Honduran congregation and several Jamaican congregations. Recently, he worshiped with an inner city congregation in the Bronx and Ghana Wesley Church in Alexandria, Virginia. He is grateful for each of these for the eye-opening insights into worship they provided and the new ways they allowed him to experience God.

You are encouraged to participate in a less familiar form of worship this week. Perhaps your congregation offers more than one style, or there are nearby churches that are part of your denomination but serve communities that are demographically different than your home church. Or you might really take a leap, and experience a service in your community that is provided by a different denomination or religious tradition altogether.

 JOURNAL REFLECTION: Reflect on your experience. How did you see God at work in this setting? What elements of worship were unfamiliar? What did you like? What, if anything, made you uncomfortable?

_____

_____

_____

_____

_____

Activity 2:
Maturing Hospitality

GOAL: Work on your own personal testimony, ready for sharing.

> *But in your hearts revere Christ as Lord. Always be prepared to give an answer to everyone who asks you to give the reason for the hope that you have. But do this with gentleness and respect. . . .*   —1 Peter 3:15 (NIV)

ACTION: We have previously engaged this Scripture, in which Peter challenges us to be ready with our words whenever and wherever they are needed. This is part of our spiritual calling as disciples. One way to do this is to have a personal testimony ready to share. We recommend a fairly simple framework:

- What was your life like before you encountered Jesus?
- How did you come to make a commitment to be a disciple of Jesus?
- What difference has Jesus made in your life?

We find a great biblical example of this in the Book of Acts, chapter 22. Please read Paul's testimony.

Using the framework provided, share your testimony. It doesn't have to be long (a page or two will do fine). Then share your testimony with someone you trust.

JOURNAL REFLECTION: What was this experience like for you? How might this prepare you for a future encounter?

_____

_____

_____

_____

_____

Activity 3:
Maturing
Being Open to Jesus

OPENING TO JESUS

GOAL: : Learn the prayer and reflection technique, Lectio Divina.

> *No, in all these things we are more than conquerors through him who loved us. For I am convinced that neither death nor life, neither angels nor demons, neither the present nor the future, nor any powers, neither height nor depth, nor anything else in all creation, will be able to separate us from the love of God that is in Christ Jesus our Lord.*
> *—Romans 8:37-39 (NIV)*

ACTION: Throughout the centuries, Christians have engaged in a type of prayerful reflection on Bible passages called Lectio Divina. The focus of this type of prayer is developing an awareness of God and God's call for our lives.

The basic framework for this type of spiritual exercise is:
- Read the text (usually a couple of times)
- Reflect on the teaching or invitation of the text
- Respond to the teaching or invitation of the text
- Rest in the assurance of God's love and power
- Record your experience

Try out this framework of prayerful reflection using Romans 8:37-39 (a portion of which is quoted above—but use the entire passage for the Lectio Divina exercise).

JOURNAL REFLECTION: Record your insights and reflections below.

_____

_____

_____

_____

Activity 4:
Maturing Obedience

OBEDIENCE

GOAL: Practice going deeper into the Scriptures with a study of the book of James.

> *For the word of God is alive and active. Sharper than any double-edged sword, it penetrates even to dividing soul and spirit, joints and marrow; it judges the thoughts and attitudes of the heart.* —Hebrews 4:12 (NIV)

ACTION: You have been introduced to a variety of study tools for your personal exploration of the Scriptures (e.g. Journalist Approach, SOAP, Lectio Divina, meditation, praying the Scriptures). Start a study on the Book of James using one or more of these tools. Take just a few verses at a time and reflect on what God is inviting you to be or do.

JOURNAL REFLECTION: Which tool or tools did you use? What observations have you made and insights have you gained so far? What is the benefit of this type of in-depth study of God's Word?

_____

_____

_____

_____

_____

_____

_____

_____

_____

Activity 5: Maturing Service

SERVICE

GOAL: Have a conversation with a community member to hear about community needs.

To answer before listening—that is folly and shame. —Proverbs 18:13 (NIV)

ACTION: One of the best ways for individuals and congregations to discover the needs of people in their community is to have conversations with people who serve the community. Schedule a visit with a community leader, a school principal, a police officer, a service organization representative, or a local business person. Take them to lunch or meet for coffee. Ask them to share what they see as the greatest needs in the community and in particular how people like you could help.

JOURNAL REFLECTION: What did you learn? What situations tugged at your heart? Was it difficult to identify a person to talk to? How did they respond to your conversation and questions? How could a church (your church) be more responsive to the needs you heard expressed?

_____

_____

_____

_____

_____

_____

_____

_____

Activity 6:
Maturing Generosity

GENEROSITY

GOAL: Consider ways to simplify your life, living as Jesus encouraged his followers.

> [Jesus speaking:] "Therefore I tell you, do not worry about your life, what you will eat or drink; or about your body, what you will wear. Is not life more than food, and the body more than clothes? Look at the birds of the air; they do not sow or reap or store away in barns, and yet your heavenly Father feeds them. Are you not much more valuable than they? Can any one of you by worrying add a single hour to your life?"
> —Matthew 6:25-27 (NIV)

ACTION: We live in a culture where we are 'wired up', 'plugged in', 'constantly connected', and bombarded with messages that encourage us to do more, have more, be more. Life has become very complicated. There are all kinds of issues associated with this lifestyle, but Jesus reminded us that life doesn't have to be that complex. We don't have to be everything and do everything. His message was to trust that God would take care of us. Read the entire passage from Matthew 6:25-34 (a portion of which is quoted above), then meditate on the ways that Jesus' words from Matthew contrast with the message with which the world is constantly bombarding us.

JOURNAL REFLECTION: How does this passage speak into your life? What step could you take this week to simplify life and trust God more?

_____

_____

_____

_____

_____

_____

MATURING

Part 3

Activity 1:
Maturing Worship

 WORSHIP

GOAL: Make time for an honest practice of Sabbath.

> *There remains, then, a Sabbath-rest for the people of God; for anyone who enters God's rest also rests from their works, just as God did from his. Let us, therefore, make every effort to enter that rest, so that no one will perish by following their example of disobedience.* —Hebrews 4:9-11 (NIV)

ACTION: From the time of the Ten Commandments, the people of God have been instructed to set aside a full day where no work was done. This was a time for connecting with God, reconnecting with family and friends, and renewing the body. The Hebrew people actually had a bunch of laws defining what was considered to be work and setting boundaries for what is known as the Sabbath.

This idea of Sabbath has been around for a very long time, but the Sabbath is still an essential practice in our hyper-busy, intensely-tethered world. Set aside a day where you commit to be untethered (no phones, ipads, computers etc.). Make it a point to spend time with your family and to connect with God. Give both your body and your mind a break.

JOURNAL REFLECTION: : What was it like to be disconnected in this way? What did you do with your family or friends? What value might there be in making this a regular practice?

_____

_____

_____

_____

_____

Activity 2:
Maturing Hospitality

HOSPITALITY

GOAL: Share a meal with a neighbor.

And [Jesus] also went on to say to the one who had invited Him, "When you give a luncheon or a dinner, do not invite your friends or your brothers or your relatives or rich neighbors, otherwise they may also invite you in return and that will be your repayment. But when you give a reception, invite the poor, the crippled, the lame, the blind, and you will be blessed, since they do not have the means to repay you; for you will be repaid at the resurrection of the righteous." —Luke 14:12-14 (NIV)

ACTION: A great way to build relationships and get to know people better is to share a meal together. Invite a neighbor (the couple next door or from down the street or the whole family) over for a meal. It doesn't have to be fancy—just a means to provide space for deeper conversation.

JOURNAL REFLECTION: What did you learn about your neighbors? What did they discover about you? How comfortable was this activity for you? How did your neighbor respond? What are the chances you will do this again?

_____

_____

_____

_____

_____

_____

_____

Activity 3:
Maturing
Being Open to Jesus

 **OPENING TO JESUS**

 GOAL: Use a reflective technique to meditate on your day.

> *May my meditation be pleasing to Him, as I rejoice in the Lord.* —Psalm 104:34 (NIV)

 ACTION: A favorite author, Ken Gire, invites us to apply a framework similar to that previously described for meditation in what he calls *The Reflective Life*. It is a way of paying attention to God in the midst of our daily routine (photographs, people we encounter, an advertisement, a movie, a newspaper article). It includes:

- Reading the moment—seeing what's on the surface.
- Reflecting on the moment—considering what's beneath the surface.
- Responding to the moment—giving what we have seen a place in our heart.

(Ken Gire, *The Reflective Life*, Chariot Victor Publishing, 1998, p. 88)

 JOURNAL REFLECTION: Pick a moment in your life and pause to reflect on it using this framework. What did you learn? How did God speak to you through this moment? How could such a reflective consideration of our day-to-day lives be an edifying regular practice?

_____

_____

_____

_____

_____

_____

_____

_____

Activity 4:
Maturing Obedience

 | OBEDIENCE

GOAL: Consider the value of mentor relationships.

And what you have heard from me in the presence of many witnesses entrust to faithful men who will be able to teach others also.
—2 Timothy 2:2 (NIV)

ACTION: One of the gifts a maturing disciple of Jesus Christ offers to the community is the willingness to help someone else also grow toward maturity. One of the ways this happens is a mentoring relationship. In a mentoring relationship (think Timothy and Paul), the mentor pours him/herself into the mentee (person being mentored). Often this relationship is based on the development of a particular skill. For example, a prayer-warrior might mentor a beginner in prayer or a person with strong financial skills might mentor someone in developing a budget.

JOURNAL REFLECTION: What do you do well (it doesn't have to be spiritual) that you could help someone learn to do or do better? Who do you know that might benefit from your expertise? What would keep you from wanting to enter in such a relationship with someone who could benefit from your skill set or experience?

_____

_____

_____

_____

_____

_____

_____

_____

Activity 5:
Maturing Service

 SERVICE

 GOAL: Consider how you might use the gift you previously identified.

> *There are different kinds of gifts, but the same Spirit distributes them. There are different kinds of service, but the same Lord. There are different kinds of working, but in all of them and in everyone it is the same God at work. Now to each one the manifestation of the Spirit is given for the common good.* —1 Corinthians 12:4-7 (NIV)

 **ACTION:** Several weeks ago you took a spiritual gifts inventory to help discern how God has uniquely gifted you. Take one of the top three gifts and consider:

- How does this line up with my other abilities?
- How does this engage my passions?
- What are some ways this gift could be used?

 JOURNAL REFLECTION: One of the best ways to confirm a particular gifting is to try it on for size. What opportunity is available through your congregation or through a local ministry or service organization for you to use this gift? Try it out! (Or if time constraints hold you back, talk to someone about a plan to try it out soon.) What are you discovering about yourself and the use of your gifts?

_____

_____

_____

_____

_____

_____

Activity 6:
Maturing Generosity

GENEROSITY

GOAL: Reflect upon Paul's journey in understanding wants, needs, and true contentment.

> *[For] I have learned to be content whatever the circumstances. I know what it is to be in need, and I know what it is to have plenty. I have learned the secret of being content in any and every situation, whether well fed or hungry, whether living in plenty or in want. I can do all this through him who gives me strength.* —Philippians 4:11-13 (NIV)

ACTION: You know the drill. If we could just have that item (car, house, boat, job) that is bigger, faster, more up-to-date, then life would be just great. And then we get it and realize there is always something bigger, faster, more up-to-date. In the passage quoted above, Paul deals with his own journey in regards to the material pressures of this world. Meditate on the lessons from his journey as they apply to yours.

JOURNAL REFLECTION: What is it that you have been longing for? How might you learn to be content with what God has already provided?

_____

_____

_____

_____

_____

_____

MATURING

~ ~ ~ ~ ~

Part 4

Activity 1:
Maturing Worship

 **WORSHIP**

 GOAL: Set up your own War Room and focus on intercessory prayer.

And pray in the Spirit on all occasions with all kinds of prayers and requests. With this in mind, be alert and always keep on praying for all the Lord's people.
—Ephesians 6:18 (NIV)

 ACTION: The movie *War Room* caught the attention of disciples across the nation across the boundaries of denominational affiliation. Although not revealed until the final scenes of the film, the power of transformed lives found its center in a place called the War Room—a place for focused prayer and intercession.

How could you create such a space in your home? Perhaps this is the space that you have already identified as your designated "time alone with God" spot based on our earlier activity. Perhaps it is just a quiet corner away from normal family activity or a rocking chair on the front porch. The key for this War Room activity is to write down and record intercessory prayer requests--to keep a record and track this need over time. Optimally, they would be somewhere that you will see them regularly. What would be helpful for you to facilitate a quiet time with God and reminders of intercessory needs? Set up a space and try it out this week.

 JOURNAL REFLECTION: What is the place you chose? Did you find it difficult to carve out time to focus on interceding for others in prayer? How did such prayer change you? How did you sense God's response and work in your life and the lives of others? How did writing the pray requests down affect your conversation with God about these requests?

_____

_____

_____

_____

_____

_____

Activity 2:
Maturing Hospitality

HOSPITALITY

GOAL: Take a field trip to a community different than your own.

There is no longer Jew or Gentile, slave or free, male and female. For you are all one in Christ Jesus. —Galatians 3:28 (NIV)

ACTION: In our current social and political culture, in which differences are emphasized and conflict between groups encouraged by many, it is important to remember the biblical mandate for people to practice empathy, understanding, and unity. In an earlier activity, we challenged you to strike up a conversation with someone who was different from you. For this activity, we are challenging you to spend time in a community that is different from your usual familiar and comfortable environment (someplace that is culturally, ethnically, racially, or socioeconomically different from where you spend most of your days). Have a meal there, worship there, participate in an activity there, or hang out with a friend who is more familiar with the area than you are.

JOURNAL REFLECTION: : What did you learn about other people? What did you learn about yourself? What was most intimidating to you about fulfilling this assignment? How do you think Jesus would have experienced this interaction? Can you think of ways to encourage more positive interaction between people who are different from one another?

Activity 3:
Maturing
Being Open to Jesus

OPENING TO JESUS

GOAL: Try fasting as a spiritual discipline.

So we fasted and petitioned our God about this, and he answered our prayer.
—Ezra 8:23 (NIV)

ACTION: Spiritual Disciplines (prayer, meditation, study, etc.) are simply ways to place us in the pathway of God's grace—to help us develop an awareness of God at work. An often ignored practice in today's culture is the discipline of fasting. Fasting is the practice of going without food for a defined period of time for the purpose of developing an awareness of God. John Wesley, the founder of the Methodist tradition, fasted weekly on Thursdays. He avoided food until mid-afternoon when he broke the fast with afternoon tea (he was British after all).

Try fasting for a day (perhaps using Wesley's approach). Each time you feel hunger pangs, remember the life that was given for you on the cross. Let the hunger pangs remind you to pay attention to God.

JOURNAL REFLECTION: What was the experience like? How did you sense the presence of God?

_____

_____

_____

_____

_____

_____

_____

Activity 4:
Maturing Obedience

 OBEDIENCE

 GOAL: Use a budget to help develop a margin that empowers generosity.

> *On the first day of every week, each one of you should set aside a sum of money in keeping with your income, saving it up, so that when I come no collections will have to be made.* —1 Corinthians 16:2 (NIV)

 ACTION: Most people seem to like the idea of being generous. But life gets in the way. We live paycheck to paycheck and spend everything we make just to make life work.

The beginning point in developing a lifestyle of generosity is to create financial margins that allow us to be generous. To make this happen, it is helpful to have a budget. Download the budget worksheet found at Kiplinger.com or another resource of your choice. Build a budget that allows you to set some resources aside for both your emergency needs and acts of generosity. Make this a family affair! We have talked about money and priorities in earlier activities, as well as giving things up so that Kingdom work might be done, but now we are putting it into a definitive spreadsheet.

 JOURNAL REFLECTION: How did your budgeting process work? What did you learn? Can you see benefits from focusing on this discipline long-term? (And if you are already a person who budgets carefully, reflect on the ways this habit relates to your stewardship practices.)

_____

_____

_____

_____

_____

_____

Activity 5:
Maturing Service

SERVICE

GOAL: Explore the second of the spiritual gifts you recently revealed (or confirmed).

> *There are different kinds of gifts, but the same Spirit distributes them. There are different kinds of service, but the same Lord. There are different kinds of working, but in all of them and in everyone it is the same God at work. Now to each one the manifestation of the Spirit is given for the common good.*
> —1 Corinthians 12:4-7 (NIV)

ACTION: Last week you referenced your completed spiritual gifts inventory and explored the application of one of your top three spiritual gifts. This week, take a second identified spiritual gift and complete the same process:

- How does this line up with my other abilities?
- How does this engage my passions?
- What are some ways this gift could be used?

JOURNAL REFLECTION: One of the best ways to confirm a particular gifting is to try it on for size. What opportunity is available through your congregation or through a local ministry or service organization for you to use this gift? Try it out! (Or if you're facing time constraints, develop a plan for trying it out or explore trying it out with a ministry leader's guidance). Then record your experience and what you learned.

_____

_____

_____

_____

_____

_____

_____

Activity 6: Maturing Generosity

 GENEROSITY

 GOAL: Explore the practice of tithing.

> *As soon as the order went out, the Israelites generously gave the firstfruits of their grain, new wine, olive oil and honey, and all that the fields produced. They brought a great amount, a tithe of everything. The people of Israel and Judah who lived in the towns of Judah also brought a tithe of their herds and flocks and a tithe of the holy things dedicated to the Lord their God, and they piled them in heaps.*
> *—2 Chronicles 31:5-6 (NIV)*

 ACTION: A spiritual practice from the most ancient of days is called tithing. This is where 10% of your income is given away to help others. Often this is given to the church, but it may also be used to support other ministries or services for which you have a passion. The tithe serves as both an opportunity to make a difference in our world and a tool to wean us from dependence on our own resources, as we learn to trust in God's provision for our needs.

Consider starting to tithe as a family. If you are unable to give a full 10%, start where you are able and raise it when finances are more under control.

 JOURNAL REFLECTION: What excites you about the possibilities of being a tithing disciple? What concerns you? (If you are already a tither, reflect on your practice of this spiritual discipline.)

_____

_____

_____

_____

_____

_____

MATURING

Part 5

Activity 1: Maturing Worship

 WORSHIP

 GOAL: Consider forming a partnership of prayer.

> *Jesus said, "For where two or three gather in my name, there am I with them."*
> *—Matthew 18:20 (NIV)*

 ACTION: Many churches have prayer teams that gather and claim that promise. It is also a promise we claim when we partner with someone and pray together. There is a special connection made with each other and with God. Spouses find that a time of prayer together is a unique bonding experience. Friends praying together find deeper relationships. Disciples praying together find a special power of prayer. Think about times when you have prayed in partnership with others. Meditate on what makes that experience different from solo prayer.

 JOURNAL REFLECTION: Who could you partner with to begin a daily time of prayer together? This could even be done by phone or email as you share prayer requests. Try a prayer partnership this week. What was the experience like?

_____

_____

_____

_____

_____

_____

_____

_____

_____

Activity 2:
Maturing Hospitality

 HOSPITALITY

 GOAL: Hang out in the community and see what you can learn.

> *The heart of the discerning acquires knowledge, for the ears of the wise seek it out.*
> *—Proverbs 18:15 (NIV)*

 ACTION: A great way to get to know people and to get a glimpse into the lives of those in your community is to hang out at a local 'watering hole' (e.g. coffee shop, diner, café). You might even consider offering to buy someone's coffee if they will share their story with you.

Spend an hour or so at a local establishment this week.

 JOURNAL REFLECTION: What did you observe about people in your community? Who did you meet? What did you learn? Did anything surprise you?

_____

_____

_____

_____

_____

_____

_____

_____

_____

Activity 3:
Maturing
Being Open to Jesus

OPENING TO JESUS

GOAL: Experience a Prayer Walk for your congregation's community.

> *The LORD said to Abram after Lot had parted from him, "Look around from where you are, to the north and south, to the east and west. All the land that you see I will give to you and your offspring forever. I will make your offspring like the dust of the earth, so that if anyone could count the dust, then your offspring could be counted. Go, walk through the length and breadth of the land, for I am giving it to you."*
> *—Genesis 13:14-17 (NIV)*

ACTION: Some weeks ago, you participated in a Prayer Walk that began at your own doorstep. Most church goers don't live within walking distance of their church home, so now we want you to engage in a Prayer Walk that begins at the church's doorstep.

Take a walk around your church's neighborhood or community, paying attention to what God wants you to see. Ask God to show you what you have failed to see previously. Ask God to give new eyes to see what has become invisible over time and new ears to hear what has become 'white noise' to us. Pay attention to the homes and how they are cared for; the cars and bumper stickers; the people you see and evidence about the lives they live; the businesses and whether they are thriving; the agencies and organizations.

JOURNAL REFLECTION: What did you see? What implications are there for meeting people's needs or making connections? Did you see things you hadn't noticed before? Did you see things that were unexpected?

_____

_____

_____

_____

_____

Activity 4:
Maturing Obedience

GOAL: Encourage somebody.

> *Therefore, encourage one another and build each other up, just as in fact you are doing.* —1 Thessalonians 5:11 (NIV)

ACTION: One of the 'one anothers' the Apostle Paul lifts up to us is this admonition to "encourage one another and build each other up."

Nancy Kline in her book, *Time to Think*, asserts that encouragement is important not because it feels good or is nice, but because it helps people to think for themselves on the cutting edge of an issue. In a culture where negativity and judgment and criticism seem to run rampant, she suggests that we aim for a 5:1 ratio of encouragement to criticism.

JOURNAL REFLECTION: Who could you encourage in some way this week? You could write a note or make a phone call or even have a personal conversation. How did it feel to offer encouragement? What was the response from the person you encouraged?

_____
_____
_____
_____
_____
_____
_____
_____
_____

Activity 5:
Maturing Service

SERVICE

GOAL: Explore the third spiritual gift you revealed.

There are different kinds of gifts, but the same Spirit distributes them. There are different kinds of service, but the same Lord. There are different kinds of working, but in all of them and in everyone it is the same God at work. Now to each one the manifestation of the Spirit is given for the common good. —1 Corinthians 12:4-7 (NIV)

ACTION: Last week you explored the second of your recently identified spiritual gifts (from the completed spiritual gifts inventory). This week, explore the third of those gifts to help discern how God has uniquely gifted you. Again, prayerfully consider the following:

- How does this line up with my other abilities?
- How does this engage my passions?
- What are some ways this gift could be used?

JOURNAL REFLECTION: One of the best ways to confirm a particular gifting is to try it on for size. What opportunity is available through your congregation or through a local ministry or service organization for you to use this gift? Try it out! (or if time constraints limit your actions at this time, brainstorm a way to try it out, or at least have a conversation with a ministry leader about trying it out). Then record your experience and what you learned.

_____

_____

_____

_____

_____

Activity 6:
Maturing Generosity

GOAL: Make an offering for a special need.

> I will make you into a great nation, and I will bless you; I will make your name great, and you will be a blessing. —Genesis 12:2 (NIV)

ACTION: We have previously encountered this story from Genesis 12, in which the idea is established that the people of God are blessed to be a blessing. There are lots of ways that we can be a blessing to others and our community. One of them is to respond financially to an identified need. In church terms we call this an offering. It is different from our tithe. An offering is a next level gift, above and beyond our regular giving, that is given to meet a particular need.

What need has been identified for you—through your church, through community organizations, through friends? How could you help meet that need?

JOURNAL RESPONSE: What did you do? How did it feel to make this kind of difference? Did you have to give something up to make this act of generosity a reality?

_____

_____

_____

_____

_____

_____

_____

MATURING

~ ~ ~ ~ ~

Part 6

Activity 1:
Maturing Worship

WORSHIP

GOAL: Help with worship leadership.

Come, let us bow down in worship, let us kneel before the Lord our Maker; for he is our God and we are the people of his pasture, the flock under his care.
—Psalm 95:6-7 (NIV)

ACTION: Experiencing the presence of God during corporate worship is an amazing gift. Usually there is a team of persons who lead up front and prepare behind the scenes to create an experience where we can be most open to God. Volunteer this week to help in leading or preparing for the worship experience. Be part of helping others experience the presence of God. You could read Scripture, lead a prayer, sing (if that's your gift), help prepare video or slides or printed material. You could even help set up or clean up.

JOURNAL REFLECTION: What did you do? How did it feel to help others experience the presence of God? Did this service affect your own experience of congregational worship? If you are already a part of worship leadership, take on a different role than usual this week. Reflect on the difference between leading worship and merely participating.

_____

_____

_____

_____

_____

_____

Activity 2:
Maturing Hospitality

GOAL: Host a neighborhood gathering or get-together.

*Let them give thanks to the Lord for his unfailing love
    and his wonderful deeds for mankind,
for he satisfies the thirsty
    and fills the hungry with good things. —Psalm 107:8-9 (NIV)*

ACTION: Our neighborhoods (whether suburban, urban, or rural) are our most readily available mission field for being and sharing the Gospel. One of the most natural ways to build connections with our neighbors is to gather together for food, fellowship, and fun. Host a block party or a cookout based around a holiday or special event, or host a bouncy house extravaganza for the kids or some other gathering that is designed to draw multiple families from the neighborhood.

If such a large gathering is too intimidating for you, host a quieter, casual dinner at which you connect some of your church friends and some of your friends or acquaintances from your neighborhood.

Gathering together is a great way to break down barriers and build relationships. Jesus even promised to be present to us in a palpable way through table fellowship.

Invite a couple of your neighbors to your home this week and enjoy an evening getting to know each other better.

JOURNAL REFLECTION: What was this experience like for you? How is sharing a meal together different from other social interactions?

_____

_____

_____

_____

Activity 3:
Maturing
Being Open to Jesus

OPENING TO JESUS

GOAL: Develop a team of spiritual advisors.

> *Without counsel plans fail, but with many advisors they succeed.*
> —*Proverbs 15:22 (NIV)*
>
> *The way of a fool is right in his own eyes, but a wise man is he who listens to counsel.*
> —*Proverbs 12:15 (NIV)*
>
> *A wise man will hear and increase in learning, and a man of understanding will acquire wise counsel.*
> —*Proverbs 1:5 (NIV)*

ACTION: A fairly common practice in the business world is to connect with an advisor or even an advisory team to receive guidance around next steps in building your business or career. These teams help us to see the bigger picture, identify obstacles, bring clarity, and even identify specific steps to greater success.

This is not a new idea. As seen in the verses quoted above, the ancient biblical wisdom from Proverbs offers the very same guidance. And it's still great advice.

JOURNAL RESPONSE: Who could serve as an advisory team for you as you seek to live into the fullness of life as a disciple of Jesus? How might you go about building such a team? Who are you using for wise guidance currently?

_____

_____

_____

_____

_____

_____

Activity 4: Maturing Obedience

OBEDIENCE

GOAL: Graduate from *Disciple* to *Discipler*.

> [Jesus speaking:] *"As you go, make disciples of all people groups, teaching them to obey". —Matthew 28:19 (Phil's translation)*

ACTION: Sometimes there is a tendency to consider our personal growth/spiritual growth as the end-game in the life as a disciple of Jesus. As important as this is, and as much focus as we have placed on this growth over the past few months, the ultimate goal is not just to make you more spiritual. It is to equip you to help others discover and grow in the love of and love *for* Jesus.

In the above passage from Matthew, Jesus could not have been any more clear: "As you go, make disciples. . . ." The commission from Jesus is to help others become disciples who grow to become more like Jesus and then help others become disciples who grow to become like Jesus, on and on in a beautiful chain of faith. You can pass along the gift you have received through this journey by becoming a Discipler for someone else.

JOURNAL RESPONSE: Who could you offer this kind of relationship to? How will you invite them? What challenges do you see lying ahead? How will you meet those challenges? Why is this important?

_____

_____

_____

_____

_____

_____

Activity 5: Maturing Service

SERVICE

GOAL: Serve your family as an expression of your discipleship.

> [H]usbands ought to love their wives as their own bodies. He who loves his wife loves himself. After all, no one ever hated their own body, but they feed and care for their body, just as Christ does the church—for we are members of his body.
> —Ephesians 5:28 (NIV)

ACTION: We often think of service as going somewhere and doing something for someone out in our neighborhoods, our cities, or the wider world. Yet, service actually starts at home. Consider Paul's words from Ephesians: Taking care of (serving) our spouses and our families is a great and high calling.

JOURNAL REFLECTION: How did you serve your family in a special way this week? How did they respond? How does your thinking about family interactions change if you think about it from this perspective of serving others as part of your call to discipleship?

_____

_____

_____

_____

_____

_____

_____

_____

Activity 6:
Maturing Generosity

 **GENEROSITY**

 GOAL: Make a stewardship vision statement.

> But godliness with contentment is great gain. For we brought nothing into the world, and we can take nothing out of it. But if we have food and clothing, we will be content with that. Those who want to get rich fall into temptation and a trap and into many foolish and harmful desires that plunge people into ruin and destruction. For the love of money is a root of all kinds of evil. Some people, eager for money, have wandered from the faith and pierced themselves with many griefs. —1 Timothy 6:6-10 (NIV)

 ACTION: Write down your vision statement for your stewardship strategy as a disciple of Jesus Christ. Write down your current attitudes and actions, then write down your goals for the future. How are you managing your income, investments, ownership, and outlays right now? What do you plan to change with God's help? Where do you want to be in five years? Ten years? What would you like to leave as your legacy when you're gone? Be as specific as you can. Write it out (optimally, with your spouse, if you are married—conceivably with your whole family participating).

 JOURNAL RESPONSE: How hard was this exercise? What truths does it force you to confront? What do you take pride in as you record your actions and attitudes? What hope does it give you moving into the future with intent? In what ways will you need to rely on God more deeply in order to see this vision to fruition?

_____

_____

_____

_____

_____

_____

_____

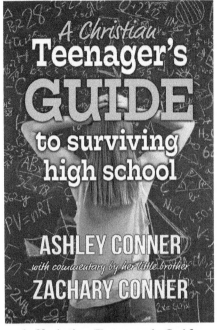
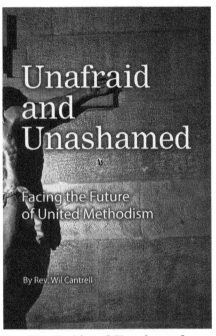
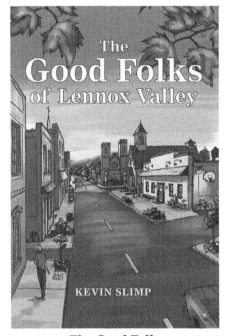

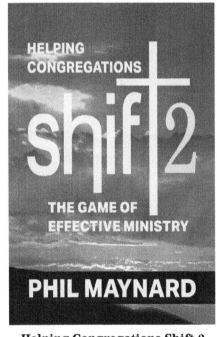